LEON

BIG SALADS

BY REBECCA SEAL

conran
OCTOPUS

First published in Great Britain in 2023
by Conran Octopus, an imprint of
Octopus Publishing Group Ltd
Carmelite House, 50 Victoria Embankment
London EC4Y 0DZ
www.octopusbooks.co.uk

An Hachette UK Company
www.hachette.co.uk

Distributed in the US by Hachette Book Group
1290 Avenue of the Americas
4th and 5th Floors, New York, NY 10104

Distributed in Canada by Canadian Manda Group
664 Annette Street, Toronto, Ontario, Canada M6S 2C8

ISBN 978-1-84091-825-0

A CIP catalogue record for this book is available from the
British Library.

Printed and bound in China

10 9 8 7 6 5 4 3 2 1

Photography by Steven Joyce

Publisher: Alison Starling
Creative director: Jonathan Christie
Senior editor: Pauline Bache
Editorial assistant: Jeannie Stanley
Copyeditor: Emily Preece-Morrison
Senior production controller: Allison Gonsalves

Food styling: Frankie Unsworth
Prop styling: Rosie Jenkins
Photography assistants: Tom Groves and Matt Hague

Key

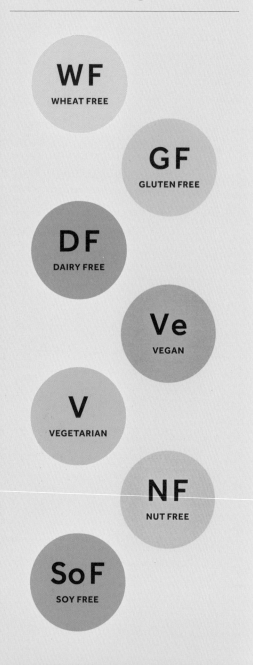

WF WHEAT FREE

GF GLUTEN FREE

DF DAIRY FREE

Ve VEGAN

V VEGETARIAN

NF NUT FREE

SoF SOY FREE

Contents

Introduction

LEON was founded to help people eat and live well. Central to this mission is getting more plants into our diets, and this book celebrates the power of plants in all their salad-y glory – every size, shape, colour and variety. Salads are good for your body, but we think they're wonderful for the soul, too. They remind us of warm, happy holidays – the table is drenched in sunlight and there's a big, beautiful bowl of deliciously-dressed leaves and vegetables in the middle, waiting for everyone to dive in.

Salads aren't just for summer, though, so you'll find a recipe for every season and occasion here. And salads are an easy way to eat a wider variety of plants. Trying to eat 30 different plants a week is a great way to do this (we easily broke that score while working on this book!). These plants could include fruits, vegetables, nuts, seeds, pulses and whole grains, eat them in addition to starchy foods, like potatoes or rice. Diversity helps create and preserve a healthy gut microbiome (another way of saying a happy, healthy community of good gut bacteria), which can lead to a more robust immune system, better brain health and even improved moods.

We hope you like making these recipes as much as we've loved creating them, and that this book leaves you excited about nourishing food that is intended to taste good and make you feel great.

We Believe In Good Food

It doesn't matter whether we're creating recipes to go in a book or dishes to serve in our restaurants, the principles are the same: we want to make it easier for everyone to eat well and live well. That means...

We like food, fast

Some of what we serve in our restaurants is familiar fast food, reimagined so it's better for you – such as our better burgers and baked fries – but we also do really good salads, smoothies, cookies, brownies, breakfasts and coffee. All of it is designed to answer our founding question: why can't fast food be good for you? In our books, we always include speedy recipes for those moments when you don't really want to cook, as well as quick fixes and the occasional delicious cheats. Life is busy, but that shouldn't mean we can't eat well.

We ♥ the Mediterranean diet

We've always loved foods from the Mediterranean diet, such as olive oil, seasonal fruits and vegetables, cheese, nuts, seeds, wholegrains and live cultured products like yoghurt and kefir. Its natural healthiness is now being backed by scientific studies into good gut health, too.

We create recipes that are inclusive

LEON is for everyone: for all ages, price points, and diets. That's why all our menus have a balance of vegetarian and vegan dishes, countering our ever-decreasing use of meat (and where we do use meat, we always ensure it is well-sourced). Whatever your dietary requirements, we want to include you and we work hard to provide options which are gluten and nut free. (We've written whole books on the topic – check out *Fast Vegan* and *Fast & Free*, our free-from cookbook.) In our recipes, we suggest swaps wherever we can, so everyone can enjoy our food. We strive to make food that suits whatever you're in the mood for, at whatever time of day. That's why we've got a breakfast menu, an all-day menu for lunch and dinner, and lots for the bits in between.

We believe in natural

The answer to almost everything can be found in nature. Our ancestors ate when they were hungry and stopped when they were full. They also lived on a diet that celebrated nature's seasonal rhythms and moved their bodies daily. We think they got it right.

We care about ingredients

Nothing goes on our menu until it passes our test: 'If a friend made it for us, would we ask them for the recipe?' In fact, many of the recipes in our books are written or inspired by our friends or members of the LEON family. Food tastes fresh when it's in season, and that's why we use and recommend cooking with seasonally ripe and local vegetables, and why we change the restaurant menus each season. We do our best to avoid additives. It means our dishes have a shorter shelf-life, but we're committed to bringing you fresh food with ingredients you can pronounce. We only buy from farms we trust. All the eggs we use are free range and all our fish is sourced from sustainable shoals. We love, and work hard, to include as many ingredients as possible that are naturally in season for restaurant menu changes. We believe that doing this provides the most flavourful dishes that our guests can enjoy and come back for time and time again.

We think food is fun

And we like to be creative with it; we scour the globe (and lots of cookbooks) to bring you new dishes you might not have eaten before. We've got room on our plates for food from all over the world, whether that's Moroccan meatballs, Brazilian black beans, Thai green curry or Korean gochujang.

We believe that happy bodies mean happy minds

Treating yourself occasionally is very important. After all, happy people are healthy people. We say: eat the treat.

How To Build A Salad
The first rule of salad club is…

…there are no rules. Unlike baking or patisserie, salads are forgiving and free-form, so if there's a combination of flavours or textures you want to try, you can. Unlike a flat cake or sunken bread, the worst that can happen with salad experimentation is that you might not like it. Want a sharper dressing, or a spicier or saltier one? Go for it. Want something warm or something crunchy or something comforting? You can have it. These pages contain a few principles that you can use as basis if you want to, but really, anything goes – as long as you like the taste.

TEXTURE IS KEY

Most of the salads we really love have an element of crisp or crunch. You can do this with croutons (including brioche, naan, chapatis or pitta), with nuts (sweet and roasted, spiced, whole, crumbled or flaked), with seeds (especially toasted and popped), with raw vegetables or fruit (radishes, chicory, celery, cucumber, pepper or apple), with roasted chickpeas, or – one of our absolute favourites – with ready-made crunch in the form of crispy onions from a packet or actual crisps (try our Chipotle Steak that includes tortilla chips on page 67).

DON'T BE AFRAID OF FRUIT

Apples and pomegranates are familiar salad ingredients, but try strawberries, raspberries, roasted or very ripe peaches or nectarines, all of which go fabulously with creamy cheeses, such as mozzarella, burrata (see page 165) or goats' cheese, along with tart flavours like balsamic vinegar, and perfumed herbs such as basil, mint or tarragon. Alternatively, use oranges or grapefruit, either sliced (see page 150), or squeezed into dressings (see pages 213 and 216).

NOT ALL SALADS ARE RAW OR COLD

In fact, very few salads taste best when they're truly cold. Where possible, bring salad ingredients, such as tomatoes, cucumber, cheese, cold meats and cured fish, to just about room temperature before serving, as cold will damp down their flavour. (Equally, be safe – don't leave food out of the fridge for long periods.) Beyond northern Europe, many countries serve cooked vegetables either warm or at room temperature and call them salads. You'll find some examples in this book (see pages 23 and 110).

GO CRAZY FOR COLOUR

We love playing with colour in our salads – but not just because we like a pretty plateful. Eating a wide range of coloured fruits and vegetables gives us the best chance of getting a variety of polyphenols into our diets. Polyphenols are useful chemicals that are involved in things such as moderating inflammation and boosting gut health. We get them from dark green vegetables, red and purple fruits and vegetables, olive oil, spices such as turmeric, herbs, nuts, seeds, coffee, some teas and dark chocolate.

WE LOVE HERBS

Even the simplest salad can be elevated with a handful of herbs: just try adding chopped fresh chives to soft lettuce and cucumber, dressed with olive oil, lemon and salt. Keeping a selection of herbs in pots on a windowsill is much better value than buying them in plastic bags.

SAVOURY-SALTY-SPICY-SOUR-SWEET

A good salad will be balanced – just sweet, salty, sour, spicy, savoury, crunchy or soft enough, with the different flavours playing together or against each other. When it comes to inventing a salad of your own, hold all this in mind.

GET DRESSED

Dressings are vital, which is why we've included one for every recipe, and more on pages 211 to 218. Some are simple, like olive oil and lemon; some are traditional, like a proper French vinaigrette (page 211); and some are spicy, funky or sour. Some have umami from soy or fish sauce, others pucker the mouth with capers or kimchi. It's hard to judge what is the most important bit of a salad, but the dressing could be it.

Salad Kit

None of these is essential, but they make salad prep easier and – looked after properly – will last a lifetime. You don't have to buy new: look for secondhand kit online or in charity shops. Most of our favourite bowls, boards and spoons came from junk shops and flea markets, and Rebecca's beloved pestle and mortar was rescued from a skip.

A JULIENNE PEELER
For shredding vegetables like carrots.

A MICROPLANE GRATER
For finely and easily grating things like ginger, garlic, Parmesan and nutmeg.

ONE REALLY BEAUTIFUL BIG BOWL
For the centre of the table.

SALAD SERVERS
Nicer and easier than using a regular fork and spoon.

CHOPPING BOARDS
Wooden chopping boards last forever, and the wood itself has antibacterial qualities. At home, we use separate boards, usually plastic, for raw meat and fish.

A SALAD SPINNER
One with a fine mesh, so you can spin chopped herbs, and a grippy bottom, so it doesn't scoot onto the floor.

A JAR WITH A LID

An old jam jar is ideal for shaking dressings and storing leftovers.

LIDDED BOXES OR BOWLS

Many of these recipes will keep for a day or two in the fridge, or can be turned into a boxed lunch. Glass boxes are heavier, but last longer and can be recycled.

A CITRUS SQUEEZER

But if you don't have one, squeeze citrus halves in your hand with the cut half facing up, so the pips don't slip into the juice.

A GOOD, SHARP KNIFE

Wash gently, keep it away from other blades and never put it in the dishwasher.

A STICK BLENDER

Choose one with a food processor attachment, so you can whizz up hummus as well as making things like mayonnaise.

A PESTLE AND MORTAR

It's always quicker to use a blender, but for some sauces (pesto, salsa verde) the results are more delicious when you grind them by hand.

KITCHEN PAPER

Not really a gadget, but if you tuck a sheet of kitchen paper inside a bag of greens or herbs when they are stored in the fridge, it will extend their life and stop them going slimy.

SPEEDY
&
SIMPLE

Crispy Pastrami

with Celeriac, Beetroot, Dill Pickles & Soft-Boiled Eggs

This is our way of turning the classic French celeriac remoulade into a more filling main course. There is something just right about earthy sweet vegetables with peppery mustard and salty, crunchy, fried pastrami. This is best served quickly, with the eggs and crispy pastrami just warm.

PREP TIME 15 MINUTES • COOK TIME 12 MINUTES

SoF / WF / GF / DF • SERVES 4

- 2 eggs
- neutral oil, for cooking
- 250g (9oz) pastrami slices, roughly torn into 2cm (¾in) pieces
- 1 celeriac (about 1kg/2lb 4oz), peeled
- 2 spring onions, finely chopped
- 4 dill pickles (pickled cucumber – choose one weighing about 40g/1½oz), sliced
- 4 ready-cooked beetroot (not in vinegar), about 250g (9oz)
- 60g (2¼oz) walnuts, roughly chopped
- finely chopped flat-leaf-parsley, to serve
- a pinch of salt and freshly ground black pepper

FOR THE DRESSING:
- 4 tablespoons good-quality mayonnaise
- 2 teaspoons wholegrain mustard
- 1 teaspoon smooth Dijon mustard
- 1 teaspoon freshly squeezed lemon juice
- 1 teaspoon sherry vinegar
- 1 teaspoon runny honey
- 1 tablespoon finely chopped fresh dill, plus extra to serve

1. Simmer the eggs in boiling water for 7½ minutes, then plunge them into cold water. When cool, peel and set aside.

2. Heat a frying pan over a medium heat. Add a splash of cooking oil and the torn pastrami and cook, in batches if necessary, shimmying the meat around the pan until crisp with frazzled edges. Remove from the heat and set aside.

3. Make the dressing by stirring together all the ingredients, being sure to disolve the honey.

4. Use a mandoline, sharp knife or box grater to finely shred the celeriac into matchsticks. Place the celeriac in a mixing bowl and add the spring onion, pickle and 2 tablespoons of the dressing. Stir until everything is coated.

5. Add 1 tablespoon of cold water to the remaining dressing, just enough to make it pourable.

6. Slice the beetroot into thin matchsticks, just like the celeriac, but don't add to the bowl (or the whole dish will turn pink).

7. Serve on a big platter or in individual portions, arranged as follows: place the celeriac mixture on the bottom, then scatter over the beetroot and walnuts. Quarter the eggs and place them on top (2 quarters per plate, if serving individually) along with the crisp pastrami. Stir the dressing again before spooning it over sparingly (you can always add more). Finish with the chopped parsley, extra dill, salt and a twist of black pepper. Eat immediately.

Beetroot with Goats' Cheese & Candied Walnuts

A classic combination, with the addition of super-easy, quick candied walnuts for a sweet crunch to go with the salty, creamy goats' cheese.

PREP TIME 10 MINUTES • COOK TIME 5 MINUTES

SoF / WF / GF / V • SERVES 4

- 60g (2¼oz) walnut pieces
- a generous knob of butter
- 2 teaspoons maple syrup
- about 400g (14oz) ready-cooked beetroot (or roast in the oven)
- about 250g (9oz) crumbly soft rindless goats' cheese
- a handful of flat-leaf parsley leaves, chopped if large
- 1 tablespoon finely chopped chives
- extra-virgin olive oil

1. Place the walnuts in a dry frying pan set over a medium heat. Toast, turning often, for 2–3 minutes, then add the butter. Once foaming, about 1 minute, toss the nuts in the butter, then remove from the heat and add the maple syrup. It will bubble, and as it does so toss the buttery nuts again to coat them in the hot syrup. Remove from the pan and set aside.

2. Cut the beetroot into small chunks and place in a serving bowl. Crumble over the cheese, then scatter over the walnuts, parsley and chives. Drizzle over a little extra-virgin olive oil, but don't toss, or the beetroot will turn the cheese pink. Eat immediately.

TIP

If your goats' cheese is mellow, rather than tangy, you might want to add a squeeze of lemon juice along with the oil, to cut through the sweet beetroot and maple-syrup nuts.

Ashley's & Stacey's Watermelon & Feta

Ashley is managing director of LEON grocery and Stacey is one of our people growth managers. When we were brainstorming salads (we love our jobs), they both suggested a watermelon and feta recipe, so we combined the two. If you want to make yours more like Stacey's, add some baby gem lettuce and leave out the basil. If you want to be more like Ashley, leave out the mint and the onion. Either way, they're both great. Just like Stacey and Ashley.

PREP TIME 10 MINUTES • COOK TIME 0 MINUTES

SoF / NF / WF / GF / V • SERVES 4

- 600g (1lb 5oz) watermelon, cubed
- 200g (7oz) feta, crumbled
- leaves from 4 bushy sprigs of fresh basil
- leaves from 2 bushy sprigs of fresh mint, torn if large
- salt and freshly ground black pepper
- ¼ red onion (or 1 shallot), very finely sliced
- extra-virgin olive oil, to serve

1. Place everything except the oil in a bowl and toss once, very gently, then pour over a splash of oil.
2. Serve immediately (Ashley likes to chill the ingredients and serve it cold from the refrigerator, but that's up to you).

TIP

Chunks of cucumber pair very well with watermelon, or add a handful of roughly chopped, pitted black olives for even more salty savouriness.

Pear, Blue Cheese, Endive & Walnuts

Bitter leaves, sweet pears, blue cheese and a mustard-y, French-style vinaigrette.
This is a very grown-up salad and a real speedy treat.

PREP TIME 15 MINUTES • COOK TIME 4 MINUTES
SoF / WF / GF / V • SERVES 4

- 50g (1¾oz) walnut pieces
- a knob of butter
- 1 teaspoon maple syrup
- 2 heads of endive/chicory (ideally 1 red and 1 white), broken into leaves, core trimmed away
- 1 pear, quartered, cored and thinly sliced lengthways
- 200g (7oz) crumbly blue cheese (we like Stilton, but any blue cheese will work)

FOR THE DRESSING:
- 1 tablespoon Dijon mustard
- 2 tablespoons rapeseed oil
- 1 teaspoon white wine vinegar
- 1 teaspoon honey
- a pinch of salt

1. Place a small pan over a medium heat. When hot, add the walnuts and butter, and cook, stirring, until the walnuts are lightly toasted and coated in the melted butter, 1–2 minutes. Remove the pan from the heat and add the maple syrup, which will foam up. Stir to coat everything again and set aside.

2. Place the endive/chicory leaves in a bowl with the pear.

3. In a separate bowl, whisk all the dressing ingredients together until smooth and emulsified, then add a splash of water to thin until pourable.

4. Spoon half of the dressing over the salad, then add the crumbled cheese and the candied walnuts and a little more dressing. Serve immediately.

Griddled Aubergine & Courgette

with Mozzarella & Pesto

Unless you have a source of really, really good-quality fresh pesto, it's best to make your own for this salad. Mint and basil are close cousins and their flavours naturally complement each other.

PREP TIME 10 MINUTES • COOK TIME 15 MINUTES

SoF / WF / GF / V • SERVES 4

- 1 aubergine, cut into 3mm (⅛in) slices on an angle
- 1 courgette, cut into 3mm (⅛in) slices on an angle
- olive oil, for cooking
- salt, to taste
- 2 balls of good-quality fresh mozzarella
- leaves from 1 bushy sprig of fresh mint, torn if large
- leaves from 2 bushy sprigs of fresh basil, torn if large
- red pepper flakes or red chilli flakes (optional)

FOR THE PESTO:

- 1 clove of garlic, crushed
- a pinch of salt
- 2 handfuls of basil leaves, roughly chopped
- leaves from 2 bushy sprigs of flat-leaf parsley, roughly chopped
- 50g (1¾oz) pine nuts
- 20g (½oz) Parmesan (check V, if needed), finely grated
- 200ml (7fl oz) extra-virgin olive oil, or as needed, plus extra to serve, if needed

1. First make the pesto: ideally, pesto is made in a pestle and mortar, but use a small food processor if time is tight. In a pestle and mortar, pummel the garlic and salt together, add the chopped herbs and pummel some more until pretty well broken down. Add the pine nuts and crush as much as you like – they give a creamy texture if broken down completely, but some like to leave them chunkier; it's up to you. Next, add the grated Parmesan and finally pour in half of the oil and mix well. Add some or all of the remaining oil until the pesto is pleasingly loose, but not runny. If using a food processor, blitz all the ingredients except the oil together, then add the oil in stages as above until you have the desired texture.

2. Place a ridged griddle pan over a medium–high heat. Brush the aubergine and courgette slices generously and thoroughly with olive oil, then lay them in a single layer in the griddle pan (you will have to do this in batches). Cook until ridge lines appear on the bottom of each piece, then turn and cook until tender throughout – the courgette can be less well cooked, but the aubergine needs to be thoroughly cooked and softened. Remove each slice from the heat, season with a little salt, and set aside while you cook the rest.

3. To serve, arrange the courgette and aubergine slices on a large platter. Tear over the mozzarella, then spoon over the pesto. Top with the fresh mint and basil leaves, a pinch of salt, and a pinch of red pepper flakes or red chilli flakes, if using.

→ *Pictured overleaf*

Sardines

with Roasted Tomatoes, Fennel & Saffron

Sardines are packed with heart-healthy Omega-3 fatty acids and are a great, sustainable fish option. This might just be the best thing we've ever done with them.

PREP TIME 10 MINUTES • COOK TIME 20–22 MINUTES

PLUS 10–15 MINUTES STANDING TIME

SoF / WF / GF / DF • SERVES 4

- 400g (14oz) cherry tomatoes, halved around the middle
- 2 heads of fennel, trimmed, cut into 1cm (½in) wedges, fronds reserved and roughly chopped for garnishing
- 3 tablespoons extra-virgin olive oil
- a pinch of salt
- a knob of butter
- 4 tablespoons pine nuts
- 4 tablespoons flaked almonds
- 2 × 125g (4½oz) cans of sardines in sunflower oil, broken into chunks
- a pinch of saffron, crumbled
- freshly ground black pepper

1. Heat the oven to 200°C fan/425°F/gas mark 7.
2. Place the cherry tomatoes and fennel wedges on a baking tray and add the oil and a pinch of salt. Use your hands to turn each piece, ensuring everything is coated in oil. Roast in the oven for 20–22 minutes, or until the tomatoes are just beginning to collapse and the fennel is charring. Set aside to cool a little.
3. Place a knob of butter in a small pan and add the pine nuts and flaked almonds. Toast for a couple of minutes, stirring often, until golden all over.
4. Place the toasted pine nuts, almonds, vegetables and the reserved chopped fennel fronds in a mixing bowl. Add the sardines and crumble over the saffron. Season with black pepper, then gently mix everything together. Leave to stand for 10–15 minutes.
5. Serve at room temperature.

⇢ *Pictured overleaf*

Whipped Ricotta

with Peas & Asparagus

This pretty salad works beautifully as a starter, arranged on individual plates. Whipping the ricotta gives it a smoother, lighter and creamier texture. You can also cut it 50:50 with feta or even a soft, rindless goats' cheese, if you prefer a bolder, saltier flavour. If you like things really cheesy, shave a little vegetarian Parmesan over the dish before eating.

PREP TIME 10 MINUTES • COOK TIME 8 MINUTES

SoF / NF / WF / GF / V • SERVES 4

- 250g (9oz) ricotta
- 2 tablespoons extra-virgin olive oil, plus extra to serve
- 1 tablespoon milk
- a pinch of salt and a twist of freshly ground black pepper, plus extra to serve
- 2 teaspoons finely chopped flat-leaf parsley
- 2 tablespoons finely chopped chives
- olive oil, for cooking
- 20 asparagus spears, trimmed
- 100g (3½oz) frozen peas
- a handful of pea shoots, rocket or lamb's lettuce
- leaves from a sprig of fresh mint, torn if large
- freshly squeezed lemon juice, to serve

1. Place the ricotta, extra-virgin olive oil and milk into the jug of a blender or a small food processor and blitz until smooth and creamy. (You can also do this by hand, with a whisk.) Stir in the salt, pepper, parsley and chives.

2. Heat a little olive oil in a large frying pan over a medium heat and add the asparagus and the peas. Sauté for a couple of minutes until the asparagus just begins to brown, shuffling it all around in the pan. Remove from the heat.

3. Divide the whipped ricotta mixture between 4 starter plates and use the back of a spoon to spread it out over the plate. Arrange the asparagus on top and scatter over the peas, then finish with the pea shoots, rocket or lamb's lettuce, plus the mint, a generous squeeze of lemon juice, a drizzle of extra-virgin olive oil and a final twist of salt and pepper.

← *Pictured previous pages*

Potato, Green Bean & Rocket
with Green Herb Pesto

The home of proper pesto is Liguria, where it is served tossed into trofie pasta with potatoes and green beans, an idea we have run with for this lovely little potato salad. We add parsley to the pesto for its robust, herbaceous flavour.

PREP TIME 15 MINUTES • COOK TIME 12 MINUTES
SoF / WF / GF / V • SERVES 4

- 500g (1lb 2 oz) new potatoes, halved or quartered if large
- salt, for the cooking water
- 100g (3½oz) green beans, trimmed and sliced on an angle into 3cm (1¼in) pieces
- a generous handful of rocket
- Parmesan shavings (check V, if needed), to serve

FOR THE PESTO:
- 1 clove of garlic, crushed
- a pinch of salt
- 2 handfuls of basil leaves, roughly chopped
- leaves from 2 bushy sprigs of flat-leaf parsley, roughly chopped
- 50g (1¾oz) pine nuts
- 20g (½oz) Parmesan (check V, if needed), finely grated
- 200ml (7fl oz) extra-virgin olive oil, or as needed, plus extra to serve, if needed

1. Cook the potatoes in boiling salted water for 12 minutes, or until tender. Add the beans to the pan for the last couple of minutes of cooking time, then drain and set aside.

2. Make the pesto: ideally, pesto is made in a pestle and mortar, but you can make it in a small food processor if you're pushed for time. In a pestle and mortar, start by pummelling the garlic and salt together, then add the chopped herbs and pummel some more until pretty well broken down. Add the pine nuts and crush as much as you like – they give a creamy texture if broken down completely, but some like to leave them chunkier; it's up to you. Next, add the grated Parmesan and finally pour in half of the oil and mix well. Add some or all of the remaining oil until the pesto is pleasingly loose, but not runny. If using a food processor, blitz all the ingredients except the oil together, then add the oil in stages as above until you have the desired texture.

3. Place the potatoes, beans and rocket in a mixing bowl. Add a few spoonfuls of the pesto and toss (you may not need all of it, or you may need it all plus some more olive oil, if the potatoes absorb the moisture from the pesto quickly). Taste for salt, then finish by shaving some Parmesan over the top. Serve promptly, as the rocket will wilt in the sauce (add the rocket and Parmesan at the last minute, if making in advance).

← *Pictured previous pages*

Mackerel Fillets
with Rainbow Slaw

Crisp fillets of mackerel on a fresh, sharp slaw. You can mix and match the root and cruciferous vegetables here – just aim for a selection of colours.

PREP TIME 20 MINUTES • COOK TIME 6 MINUTES

SoF / NF / WF / GF / DF • SERVES 4

- olive oil, for cooking
- 4 mackerel fillets
- salt and freshly ground black pepper

FOR THE SLAW:
- 75g (2½oz) carrot, cut into fine matchsticks, or coarsely grated
- 50g (1¾oz) white cabbage, shredded
- 50g (1¾oz) red cabbage, shredded
- 1 medium beetroot, peeled and cut into fine matchsticks, or coarsely grated
- 50g (1¾oz) celeriac, peeled and cut into fine matchsticks, or coarsely grated
- 75g (2½oz) fennel, shredded
- 1 spring onion, halved lengthways and very finely chopped
- a handful of flat-leaf parsley
- leaves from 4 bushy sprigs of dill
- 1 orange, halved
- 1 tablespoon extra-virgin olive oil
- salt, to taste

1. First, make the slaw: place all the vegetables and herbs in a large mixing bowl. Cut the peel and pith away from half of the orange and chop the flesh into small pieces. Add the flesh to the bowl.

2. Squeeze the other half of the orange almost completely into a small bowl (keep a little back to squeeze over the fish) and add the extra-virgin olive oil and a pinch of salt. Whisk to combine, then pour over the slaw. Toss gently.

3. Cook the mackerel: place a frying pan over a high heat and add a splash of oil. Pat the fish fillets dry using kitchen paper and season all over with salt and pepper. Place into the hot pan, skin-side down, and cook for 2–3 minutes, or until the skin is crispy. Turn and cook the other side for 2–3 minutes until just cooked through.

4. Serve the fish hot, perched on top of the slaw, with a final squeeze of orange juice over each fillet.

LEON's
Quinoa, Feta & Greens

*This is inspired by a salad that still sometimes appears on our menu,
the New Original Salad, which started life at the same time LEON did, in the mid 2000s.
We sell a similar salad in supermarkets, Greens and Grains, that also includes pumpkin seeds
and added edamame beans.*

PREP TIME 15 MINUTES • COOK TIME 20 MINUTES

SoF / NF / WF / GF / V • SERVES 4

- 50g (1¾oz) quinoa
- 125g (4½oz) frozen peas
- 125g (4½oz) broccoli, cut into small florets
- 1 tablespoon sunflower seeds
- 1 tablespoon linseeds
- 125g (4½oz) cucumber, diced
- 3 large cos lettuce leaves (or 6–7 gem lettuce leaves), chopped into small pieces
- a generous handful of spinach
- a big handful of flat-leaf parsley leaves
- leaves from 2 sprigs of fresh mint
- leaves from 2 sprigs of fresh basil
- 200g (7oz) feta, crumbled

FOR THE DRESSING:

- 2 tablespoons Dijon mustard
- 4 tablespoons sunflower or rapeseed oil
- 2 teaspoons white wine vinegar
- a generous pinch of salt

1. Place the quinoa in a pan and cover with 150ml (5fl oz) cold water. Bring to a simmer and cook for about 20 minutes, or until tender (or according to the packet instructions). Drain and set aside to cool.

2. Meanwhile, place the peas and broccoli in a pan of freshly boiled water. Bring back to the boil, then drain and set aside.

3. In a bowl, whisk together the dressing ingredients until smooth.

4. Toast the seeds in a hot dry pan, until golden, about 1 minute. Tip into a large bowl, then add the cooled quinoa, peas, broccoli, cucumber, lettuce, spinach and herbs. Add half of the dressing and toss well.

5. Finally, add the feta and the remaining dressing and toss once gently – don't mix too vigorously or the feta will fall apart. Serve immediately.

Yoghurt, Herb & Macaroni

Moro is a long-standing favourite restaurant of Rebecca's. Her first visit was as a student and she still goes regularly. Married founders and chefs Sam and Sam Clark have also written several brilliant cookbooks (Rebecca owns them all). This is a version of their inspired macaroni yoghurt salad – and one of the very few pasta salads Rebecca considers worth the effort.

PREP TIME 10 MINUTES • **COOK TIME 7 MINUTES**

SoF / V • **SERVES 4 AS A SIDE**

- 100g (3½oz) macaroni
- a generous pinch of salt, plus extra for the cooking water
- a knob of butter
- 2 tablespoons pine nuts
- 1 clove of garlic, crushed
- 2 tablespoons finely chopped flat-leaf parsley
- 2 tablespoons finely chopped fresh coriander
- 1 tablespoon extra-virgin olive oil
- 4 heaped tablespoons thick Greek style yoghurt (or plant-based alternative)
- a pinch of dried red chilli flakes
- a generous pinch of baharat spice blend or Lebanese 7-spice blend (or mix a little ground allspice with ground cumin, ground coriander and ground cinnamon)
- 2 teaspoons lemon juice, plus extra as needed

1. Cook the macaroni in a pan of boiling salted water for about 7 minutes, or until al dente. Drain and place in a mixing bowl.
2. Place a small pan over a medium heat and add the butter. When foaming, add the pine nuts and garlic, and cook for just a minute or two until the pine nuts are golden. Add to the bowl with the macaroni.
3. Add all the other ingredients to the bowl and stir well. Taste, adding more salt, lemon or spice until you are happy with the seasoning. Eat immediately.

TIP

Add crumbled feta for more tang, or diced cucumber and chopped dill for a fresher take.

Pan-fried Fish Caesar

*The Caesar bit of a Caesar salad is just the greens, croutons, dressing and Parmesan,
so you can technically use whatever you like as protein. Here, pan-fried fish fillets work
wonderfully with our classic anchovy-heavy dressing.*

PREP TIME 15 MINUTES • COOK TIME 20 MINUTES

SoF / NF • SERVES 4

- 300g (10½oz) ciabatta, torn into chunks
- 4 tablespoons extra-virgin olive oil
- 1 cos lettuce (or similar crisp lettuce), large leaves torn or chopped
- a generous handful of flat-leaf parsley leaves
- a small bunch of chives, roughly chopped, plus extra, finely chopped, to garnish
- 4 skin-on fish fillets (mackerel is great, or use sea bass or red mullet if you prefer a more subtle flavour), patted dry
- vegetable oil, for cooking
- salt and freshly ground black pepper
- Parmesan shavings (optional)

FOR THE DRESSING:
- 3 egg yolks
- 2 teaspoons Dijon mustard
- 2 teaspoons freshly squeezed lemon juice
- a dash of Worcestershire sauce
- 10 anchovies in oil, finely chopped
- 1 clove of garlic, crushed
- 2 tablespoons olive oil
- 100ml (3½fl oz) neutral vegetable oil
- water, to loosen

1. Heat the oven to 175°C/375°F/gas mark 5.
2. Place the bread and olive oil on a baking tray and toss to coat. Cook in the oven for 20 minutes, until golden and crisp.
3. For the dressing, beat together the egg yolks and mustard in a food processor, then add the lemon juice, Worcestershire sauce, anchovies and garlic. Blitz until completely smooth. Add the olive oil, 1 tablespoon at a time, blending after each addition. When it's completely incorporated, add the vegetable oil, a quarter at a time, blending with each addition to a mayo-like consistency. Store half of the mixture in a sealed container in the refrigerator, for another meal. Place the other half in a small bowl and slowly add 2–3 teaspoons of cold water, mixing well after each addition, until you have a thick but pourable dressing. Set aside.
4. Place the lettuce, parsley, chives and croutons in a mixing bowl. Gradually add half of the dressing and toss thoroughly.
5. Season the fish all over. Place a frying pan over a medium heat and add a splash of oil. When hot, add the fish, skin-side down. Cook until the skin begins to blister and brown, then turn and cook for another 2 minutes until cooked through. Remove from the heat and halve the fillets.
6. Divide the salad between 4 plates and arrange the fish on top. Drizzle a little more dressing over the fish. Use a peeler or grater to shave flakes of Parmesan, if using, over each serving and garnish with a pinch of the finely chopped chives.

Figs with Mozzarella, Rocket & Balsamic

This salad is beautifully simple, but also very customizable: try it with ricotta rather than mozzarella (or feta, or your favourite good-quality dairy-free cheese); add basil as well as rocket; top with crisped-up prosciutto; swap the walnuts for toasted almonds; dress with honey instead of balsamic... It's worth getting the mozzarella out of the refrigerator well in advance of making this, so that it's not stone-cold in contrast to the room-temperature figs.

PREP TIME 5 MINUTES • COOK TIME 0 MINUTES
SoF / WF / GF / V • SERVES 4

- 2 big handfuls of rocket
- 4 ripe figs, quartered
- 3 tablespoons chopped walnuts
- 2 balls of good-quality buffalo mozzarella, torn into bite-sized pieces
- 1 tablespoon balsamic vinegar
- 2 tablespoons extra-virgin olive oil
- a pinch of salt

1. Arrange the rocket in the bottom of a wide serving bowl. Top with the quartered figs, walnuts and torn mozzarella.
2. In a separate bowl, whisk together the balsamic vinegar, olive oil and salt, then drizzle this dressing over the salad. Eat immediately.

→ *Pictured overleaf*

Ashley's Lemon Cauliflower
with Herbs & Pomegranate

Surprisingly easy and deceptively delicious, this salad belongs to Ashley,
managing director of LEON grocery.

PREP TIME 10 MINUTES • COOK TIME 0 MINUTES
PLUS 20 MINUTES MARINATING

SoF / NF / WF / GF / DF / V / Ve • SERVES 4

- 400g (14oz) raw cauliflower (1 medium), finely chopped
- juice of ½ lemon
- a generous pinch of salt
- leaves from 4 bushy sprigs of mint, chopped
- leaves from 4 bushy sprigs of flat-leaf parsley, chopped
- 1 tablespoon extra-virgin olive oil
- 5 tablespoons pomegranate seeds

1. Tip the chopped cauliflower into a bowl, then add the lemon juice and salt. Mix well, then set aside for 20 minutes to marinate.
2. When ready to serve, add all the other ingredients and toss.

→ *Pictured overleaf*

TIP
This is lovely on the side of roasted chicken or roasted vegetables with a dollop of aioli (page 216 or page 215 for vegan) or dairy or vegan yoghurt.

Trout, Edamame & Seaweed

It's now easy to get a wide range of dried seaweeds, which are great for making salads. We get ours online from the Japan Centre. If you can't find arame, use any seaweed salad mix – but check the packet for quantities, as some increase in size by up to 10 times as they rehydrate.

PREP TIME 15 MINUTES PLUS SOAKING • COOK TIME 14 MINUTES
NF / WF / GF / DF • SERVES 4

- 15g (½oz) dried arame seaweed
- 3 generous pinches of dried wakame seaweed
- 4 eggs
- 200g (7oz) frozen, shelled edamame beans
- oil, for cooking
- 4 trout fillets
- 50g (1¾oz) cucumber, finely sliced
- 2 spring onions, finely chopped

FOR THE DRESSING:
- 2 tablespoons tamari soy sauce (check WF/ GF, if needed)
- 2 tablespoons mirin
- 2 tablespoons sesame oil

1. Rehydrate the arame seaweed and the wakame seaweed separately, according to the packet instructions.
2. Simmer the eggs in boiling water for 7½ minutes, then plunge them into cold water, to stop them cooking. When cool enough to handle, peel and set aside.
3. Return the egg pan to the heat and add the edamame beans to the simmering water. Return to the boil, cook for 2 minutes, then drain and set aside.
4. Place a frying pan over a medium heat and add a splash of oil. When hot, sauté the trout fillets for 1–2 minutes per side until just cooked through.
5. Stir together the dressing ingredients.
6. Drain the seaweeds and arrange on 4 plates. Slice the eggs in half and add to the plates. Top with the edamame beans, cucumber and spring onions, then add the cooked trout fillets. Spoon over the dressing and serve immediately.

Gyoza & Crunchy Slaw

Gyoza are Japanese pan-fried dumplings. Although it is possible to buy them fresh, they are more easily available frozen. Lots of supermarkets do good gyoza, but we especially like the slightly harder-to-find Ajinomoto brand. They work brilliantly perched on this crunchy, spicy slaw.

PREP TIME 15 MINUTES • COOK TIME 8 MINUTES
NF / DF / V / Ve • SERVES 4

- 125g (4½oz) Chinese leaf, finely shredded
- 175g (6oz) white cabbage, finely shredded
- 2 spring onions, finely chopped
- 100g (3½oz) carrots (ideally a range of colours), shredded or cut into matchsticks
- 100g (3½oz) radishes, finely sliced
- a generous handful of fresh coriander leaves
- 3 tablespoons vegan mayonnaise (or regular)
- 2 teaspoons soy sauce
- 4–6 vegetable gyoza (fresh or frozen) per person, depending on their size
- vegetable oil, for cooking
- 3 tablespoons crispy onions from a packet
- a pinch of roasted/toasted sesame seeds
- sriracha sauce, to serve

FOR THE DRESSING:

- 3 tablespoons toasted sesame oil
- 1 tablespoon finely chopped red chilli
- 1 small clove of garlic, crushed
- 1 small thumb of ginger, peeled and finely grated
- 1 teaspoon soy sauce
- 1 tablespoon lime juice
- 1 teaspoon soft brown sugar
- 1 teaspoon miso paste

1. Stir together the dressing ingredients, mashing the miso paste into the mixture until completely incorporated.
2. Tip all the vegetables and coriander leaves into a large mixing bowl, then pour the dressing over and toss well to coat.
3. Stir together the vegan mayo and soy sauce in a small bowl. Add a splash of water to make the mayo pourable.
4. To cook the gyoza, set a frying pan with a lid over a medium heat and pour in a splash of oil. When hot, add the gyoza, placing them flat-side down into the oil. Cook for 2–3 minutes until golden on the bottom (or follow the packet instructions), then add a couple of tablespoons of water to the pan and quickly cover with a lid. Steam the gyoza for 4 minutes, then remove from the heat.
5. Divide the slaw between 4 wide shallow bowls and perch the gyoza on top. Scatter over the crispy onions and a pinch of sesame seeds. Drizzle over the soy mayo and then zig-zag over the sriracha. Eat immediately.

TIP

The slaw will keep for a couple of days in the refrigerator and is great on the side of dishes like crispy tofu or bao buns.

Tenderstem Broccoli
with Almonds & Jammy Eggs

A lovely way to get more greens (or purples if you manage to get our favourite, purple sprouting broccoli) onto your plate.

PREP TIME 5 MINUTES • COOK TIME 12 MINUTES
SoF / WF / GF / V • SERVES 4

- **3 eggs**
- **300g (10½oz) Tenderstem or purple sprouting broccoli**
- **100g (3½oz) butter**
- **4 tablespoons flaked almonds**
- **a pinch of salt**

1. Simmer the eggs in boiling water for 7½ minutes, then plunge them into cold water, to stop them cooking. When cool enough to handle, peel and cut each egg into 4 wedges. Set aside.

2. Steam the broccoli (you can do this over the eggs if you have a steamer basket) in a lidded pan filled with 3cm (1in) water until tender. This should take no more than 3–4 minutes. Remove from the heat and set aside.

3. Working quickly, set a small frying pan over a medium heat and add the butter. When melted, add the flaked almonds. Meanwhile, arrange the broccoli and egg wedges on a serving plate. As soon as the almond pieces turn brown, tip the contents of the pan over the broccoli and eggs, carefully ensuring every piece of broccoli gets a good covering of butter and almonds.

4. Scatter over a pinch of salt and serve right away – the eggs shouldn't be cold and the butter will thicken up if not eaten immediately.

TIP
Make this vegan: ditch the eggs, use olive oil instead of butter and serve with the Tahini Sauce on page 176.

Bread & Egg Salad

This simply tastes of summer. Bright and crispy,
but still very substantial.

PREP TIME 15 MINUTES • COOK TIME 10 MINUTES

SoF / NF / DF • SERVES 4

- 200g (7oz) day-old ciabatta, torn into croutons
- 4 tablespoons extra-virgin olive oil (choose one that is mild and not bitter)
- 3 eggs
- 1 tablespoon cider vinegar
- 300g (10½oz) juicy and ripe tomatoes (ideally different shapes, sizes and colours), chopped into rough 2cm (¾in) pieces
- 1 shallot, very finely sliced
- 3 anchovies, finely chopped
- 1 tablespoon capers in brine, drained and roughly chopped
- leaves from 2 bushy sprigs of basil, torn if large
- leaves from 2 bushy sprigs of flat-leaf parsley, roughly chopped if large
- 1 sustainably sourced avocado (available online or try a 'wonky' veg box), cut into rough chunks (optional)

1. First, make the croutons: heat the oven to 200°C fan/425°F/ gas mark 7. Place the ciabatta pieces on a baking tray and spoon over 2 tablespoons of the extra-virgin olive oil. Use your hands to toss, so that each piece is lightly coated, then bake in the oven for 10 minutes until golden and crisp.

2. Meanwhile, simmer the eggs in boiling water for 7½ minutes, then plunge them into cold water, to stop them cooking. When cool enough to handle, peel and set aside.

3. Place the remaining 2 tablespoons of oil, the cider vinegar, tomatoes, shallot, anchovies, capers, basil and parsley in a serving bowl and toss. Add the avocado (if using) and croutons, and gently toss once more – don't bash the avocado up or it will turn to mush. Slice each egg into 4 wedges and arrange on top of the salad.

Hearts of Palm
with Mayo, Chives & Brioche Croutons

The flavours in this are inspired by the classic New England lobster roll, but – given that it contains no lobster – it's considerably cheaper. (Of course, if you want to splash out on seafood, go ahead!) Hearts of palm come in cans, and are salty, white and tender, making them a great sub for seafood. (They can smell a bit weird when you open the can – just rinse, if so.)

PREP TIME 10 MINUTES • COOK TIME 6 MINUTES

SoF / NF / V • SERVES 4

- 200g (7oz) brioche
- butter, for spreading
- 175g (6oz) canned hearts of palm, drained, rinsed and roughly chopped
- 2 celery sticks, finely diced
- 1 head of soft lettuce (round or butterhead), broken into leaves and torn, if large
- 4 tablespoons finely chopped chives
- freshly squeezed lemon juice
- salt and freshly ground black pepper

FOR THE SAUCE:
- 4 tablespoons mayonnaise (or vegan mayo)
- ¼ teaspoon cayenne pepper

1. Heat the oven to 200°C fan/425°F/gas mark 7.
2. Butter the brioche, then cut it into 2cm (¾in) cubes. Place the cubes on a baking tray, buttered-side up, and bake for 6 minutes, or until beginning to brown. Remove and set aside.
3. Divide the hearts of palm, celery and lettuce between 4 plates. Scatter over the chives and squeeze over a little lemon juice. Season lightly with salt and freshly ground black pepper.
4. Stir the mayo and cayenne together and add a little splash of water, just enough to make it spoonable but still thick. Spoon about half of the sauce over the salad.
5. Eat immediately, with the remaining sauce available for anyone who wants more.

Tabbouleh

For proper, traditional tabbouleh you need lots and lots of parsley –
it's often made with more bulgur wheat than parsley, when really it should be
the other way around. Using a mixture of flat-leaf and curly parsley works really well,
because the flavour of curly parsley is more intense.

PREP TIME 10 MINUTES • COOK TIME 20 MINUTES

SoF / NF / DF / V / Ve • SERVES 4

- 50g (1¾oz) bulgur wheat
- 3 extra large handfuls of curly parsley, very finely chopped
- 4 extra large handfuls of flat-leaf parsley, very finely chopped
- leaves from 2 bushy sprigs of fresh mint, very finely chopped
- ¼ red onion, very finely chopped
- 75g (2½oz) cherry or very ripe tomatoes, very finely chopped
- 2 pinches of ground allspice
- 2–3 tablespoons extra-virgin olive oil
- 2–3 teaspoons lemon juice
- salt

1. Cook the bulgur wheat according to the packet instructions (usually bulgur is simmered in salted boiling water for 12–15 minutes until tender, or you can cover it in boiling water, place a lid on top, and leave to absorb for about 20 minutes). Drain and spread over a plate to cool.
2. Place the chopped herbs, red onion, tomatoes and cooled bulgur in a large mixing bowl. Add the allspice, 2 tablespoons of the extra-virgin olive oil and 2 teaspoons of the lemon juice, plus a pinch of salt. Toss and then taste, adding more oil, lemon, salt or allspice, as needed.

→ *Pictured overleaf*

TIP

The salad should be mainly parsley, flecked throughout with bulgur, and it should taste very fresh and just a little bit tart. Tabbouleh is best eaten on the day it is made, as otherwise the parsley will begin to lose its brilliant green colour.

Pinar's Gavurdağı Salatası

This amazing courgette salad is courtesy of our colleague Pinar Seseogullari, who works in Hammersmith LEON but hails from Turkey. Gavurdağı salatası is a tomato and walnut salad, spiked with sour sumac. For this, the most important part is to chop the vegetables as small as possible.

PREP TIME 15 MINUTES • COOK TIME 0 MINUTES

SoF / WF / GF / DF / V / Ve • SERVES 4

- 5 baby cucumbers (sometimes called Lebanese cucumbers)
- 4 ripe plum tomatoes (or similar)
- 2 green peppers
- 1 large handful of flat-leaf parsley leaves
- 1 red onion
- 6 tablespoons extra-virgin olive oil
- 4 tablespoons pomegranate molasses
- 1 teaspoon sumac
- ½ teaspoon salt
- 100g (3½oz) walnut pieces

1. First, peel the cucumbers, then dice them, as well as the tomatoes, green peppers (removing the seeds and ribs), parsley and onion.
2. Place everything in a large bowl and mix with the olive oil, pomegranate molasses, sumac and salt.
3. Serve with the walnut pieces scattered on top.

→ *Pictured overleaf*

Roast Broccoli

with Tahini Yoghurt & Pistachios

*There is something mystical about the combination of broccoli and tahini –
it's one of our favourites.*

PREP TIME 10 MINUTES • COOK TIME 8 MINUTES

SoF / WF / GF / V • SERVES 4

- 250g (9oz) purple sprouting broccoli
- 1–2 tablespoons olive oil, for cooking
- a pinch of salt
- pomegranate molasses, for drizzling
- 1 tablespoon shelled pistachios, roughly chopped and toasted
- a pinch of toasted sesame seeds

FOR THE TAHINI YOGHURT:
- 7 heaped tablespoons thick Greek-style yoghurt (or plant-based alternative)
- 1½ tablespoons light tahini
- 1 tablespoon lemon juice
- 1 tablespoon extra-virgin olive oil, plus extra to serve
- a pinch of salt

1. Heat the oven to 200°C fan/425°F/gas mark 7.
2. Place the broccoli on a baking tray and pour over the oil, then massage it along with the salt into the florets. Roast in the oven for 6 minutes.
3. Meanwhile, stir together the tahini yoghurt ingredients in a bowl (the tahini may be lumpy, so just keep stirring until it's smooth). Taste and add more salt or lemon juice, as needed.
4. Serve on a wide plate. Spread the tahini yoghurt in a thick swirl across the plate, then arrange the roast broccoli on top. Drizzle over a little pomegranate molasses and a little more extra-virgin olive oil. Finally, sprinkle over the pistachios and toasted sesame seeds.

← *Pictured previous pages*

Pinar's Kabak Tarator

Another delicious recipe from our Turkish
LEON colleague Pinar Seseogullari (see page 51).

PREP TIME 10 MINUTES • COOK TIME 5 MINUTES
SoF / NF / WF / GF / V • SERVES 4 WITH OTHER DISHES

- 1 tablespoon extra-virgin olive oil, plus extra to serve
- 1 medium courgette, coarsely grated
- 250g (9oz) Greek-style yoghurt (or plant-based alternative)
- ½ a small bunch of dill, finely chopped, plus some extra sprigs to serve
- 1 clove of garlic, crushed or finely chopped
- ½ teaspoon freshly ground black pepper
- ½ teaspoon salt

1. Pour the oil into a wide pan set over a medium heat. When hot, add the grated courgette and cook, stirring often, until it softens but doesn't brown, for about 5 minutes. Add salt and pepper and cook for a further minute. Remove from the heat and leave to cool.
2. In a bowl, mix together the yoghurt, dill and garlic, then add the cooled courgettes and mix gently.
3. Just before serving, spoon a little more olive oil on top and add the extra sprigs of dill.

← *Pictured previous pages*

TIP

You can make this with a mixture of grated carrots and courgette – cook the carrots down first and garnish with toasted walnuts.

Herbed Potato & Feta

The flavours here remind Rebecca of a happy time she spent researching a cookbook in Greece. This works just as well without the capers and olives, so if they're not your favourites, leave them out.

PREP TIME 15 MINUTES • COOK TIME 12 MINUTES

SoF / NF / WF / GF / V • SERVES 4 AS A SIDE

- 400g (14oz) waxy new potatoes, chopped into quarters
- salt, for the cooking water
- ¼ red onion (or 1 shallot), very finely sliced
- 150g (5½oz) feta, crumbled
- 4 tablespoons finely chopped flat-leaf parsley
- 4 tablespoons finely chopped fresh mint
- a generous pinch of dried oregano (or 1 tablespoon finely chopped fresh oregano)
- 2 tablespoons capers in brine, drained and roughly chopped if large (optional)
- 10 pitted kalamata olives, roughly chopped (optional)
- freshly squeezed lemon juice, to taste
- 3 tablespoons extra-virgin olive oil
- freshly ground black pepper

1. Cook the potatoes in boiling salted water until tender to the point of a knife, about 12 minutes. Drain and leave to cool slightly.

2. Place the potatoes in a bowl with all the other ingredients and toss. Taste, adding more lemon juice, olive oil or pepper, as needed (you probably won't need salt, as feta is salty). Serve.

Dakos Salad

Dakos are barley rusks topped with grated tomato and Cretan cheese, mizithra. This recipe deconstructs that dish and uses ciabatta and feta, as they're easier to get hold of than rusks and mizithra. Nonetheless, the flavour takes Rebecca straight back to working on a book in Crete, a few years ago. Some cooks like to load their dakos with olives, peppers, capers or parsley, but the majority of Cretan dakos (and similar dishes served elsewhere in the Greek islands) are made with nothing more than tomatoes, cheese and oregano.

PREP TIME 10 MINUTES • COOK TIME 20 MINUTES

SoF / NF / V • SERVES 4

- 150g (5½oz) ciabatta, torn into croutons
- 2 tablespoons extra-virgin olive oil
- 500g (1lb 2oz) tomato flesh, peeled and coarsely grated (discard the skins)
- a pinch of salt
- a generous pinch of dried oregano
- 200g (7oz) feta, crumbled
- fresh oregano leaves, to serve

1. Heat the oven to 175°C fan/375°F/gas mark 5.
2. Place the bread and olive oil on a baking tray and use your hands to toss the bread in the oil. Bake in the oven for 15–20 minutes, or until golden and crisp.
3. Place the grated tomato and a pinch of salt in a bowl. Add the ciabatta croutons and dried oregano and toss.
4. Serve on individual plates, with the tomato mixture on the bottom, some crumbled feta on top and a few oregano leaves on each portion.

TIP

For crunchy croutons, assemble this just before serving, or they will soften and become soggy.

Niçoise

*Rebecca once wrote an article about the history of the Niçoise salad for 'National Geographic',
so she's only too aware of the controversies swirling around how to make it – arguments
that have now been raging for a century. This version is pared back and probably quite similar
to the earliest ways it was made: lots of tomatoes, no croutons, no potatoes, no green beans,
no spring onions, no lettuce. But it's your salad, so do what you like – add any of the above,
plus some artichoke hearts if you fancy.*

PREP TIME 15 MINUTES • COOK TIME 7½ MINUTES

SoF / NF / DF • SERVES 4

- 3 eggs
- 500g (1lb 2oz) ripe plum tomatoes, chopped into rough 2cm (¾in) pieces
- 200g (7oz) certified sustainable albacore/skipjack tuna in sunflower or olive oil, drained and crumbled into chunks
- 10 good-quality black olives, pitted and quartered
- 8 anchovies, sliced thinly on an angle into long pieces
- 1 tablespoon Dijon mustard
- 2 teaspoons red wine vinegar
- 4 tablespoons extra-virgin olive oil
- 2 tablespoons very finely chopped chives
- 2 tablespoons very finely chopped flat-leaf parsley
- crusty French-style bread, to serve

1. Simmer the eggs in boiling water for 7½ minutes, then plunge them into cold water, to stop them cooking. When cool enough to handle, peel and set aside.
2. Arrange the tomatoes, tuna, olives and anchovies on a serving platter.
3. In a bowl, stir together the mustard and red wine vinegar, then slowly add the olive oil, whisking to form a smooth emulsion. Stir in the chopped herbs and add a dash of water, if needed, to thin the dressing slightly.
4. Slice the eggs into 4 wedges and arrange on top of the salad, then spoon over the dressing. Serve the salad (ideally in the Provençal sunshine) with crusty bread on the side.

Beetroot, Halloumi, Rocket & Peppers

Credit for this belongs to Steve, Rebecca's husband (and the photographer for this book), who managed to make something out of nothing one Saturday lunchtime, when it appeared there was only half a bunch of muddy beetroot and a bag of rocket in the refrigerator. Yellow, orange or candied beetroot look prettiest alongside red and yellow roasted peppers, if you can get hold of them.

PREP TIME 15 MINUTES • COOK TIME 4 MINUTES

SoF / NF / WF / GF / V • SERVES 4

- 2 big handfuls of rocket
- 4 small candied beetroot, peeled and finely sliced into rounds
- 2 roasted peppers from a jar, sliced
- vegetable or rapeseed oil, for cooking
- 1 block of halloumi (about 200g/7oz), broken into 1–2cm (½–¾in) pieces
- extra-virgin olive oil, to serve
- lemon juice, to serve

1. Arrange the salad first, as cooked halloumi quickly becomes rubbery as it cools. Strew the rocket on plates or a platter, then arrange the sliced beetroot and roasted peppers among it.

2. Set a frying pan over a medium heat and add a splash of cooking oil. Pat the halloumi dry (so that it doesn't cause splatters in the pan) using kitchen paper, then place in the pan and fry for about 2 minutes on each side, or until golden brown. Remove from the heat and dot the halloumi around the salad.

3. Spoon over a little extra-virgin olive oil and some lemon juice (halloumi is very salty, so you probably won't need salt), then serve.

HOT
&
SPICY

Chipotle Steak
with Griddled Spring Onions

Spicy, sour, crunchy and fiery, with the sweetness of fresh corn – this salad has it all.

PREP TIME 16 MINUTES • COOK TIME 12 MINUTES

SoF / NF / WF / GF / DF • SERVES 4

- vegetable or rapeseed oil, for cooking
- 2 teaspoons chipotle paste
- 2 corn-on-the-cob
- 6 spring onions, trimmed and sliced on an angle into 4cm (1½in) pieces
- 225g (8oz) sirloin or rump steak, fat trimmed, sliced to about 3cm (1in) thick
- a handful of tortilla chips (check GF, if needed)
- 2 tablespoons pumpkin seeds, toasted in a dry pan

FOR THE DRESSING:
- 1 teaspoon chipotle paste
- 3 tablespoons extra-virgin olive oil
- 2 tablespoons vegetable or rapeseed oil
- juice of 1 lime
- 1 shallot, very finely diced
- 2 teaspoons honey
- 1 teaspoon sherry vinegar
- ¼ teaspoon ground cumin
- a generous pinch of salt and lots of freshly ground black pepper

FOR THE SALAD:
- 1 head of cos lettuce, chopped into bite-sized pieces
- a large handful of lamb's lettuce
- 8 radishes, finely sliced
- a large handful of fresh coriander leaves
- 1 ripe tomato, finely chopped

1. Whisk together all the dressing ingredients. Taste – it should be sharp, sweet, spicy and just a little bit salty, all at once. Set aside.

2. Place all the salad ingredients in a large bowl, spoon 2 tablespoons of the dressing over and toss well.

3. Set a frying pan over a medium heat and add a splash of cooking oil. Mix together the chipotle paste and a further 1 tablespoon of oil in a small bowl, then brush or spoon half of it over the corn cobs. Place the cobs and spring onions in the hot pan and cook, turning often, until the corn begins to blister and brown in places and the spring onions begin to char (turn on your extractor fan if you have one as the chilli will spread into the air!). Remove from the heat. When cool enough to handle, use a sharp knife to slice the corn kernels off the cob.

4. Keep the pan on the heat. Brush the steak with the remaining chipotle mixture and sear in the hot pan until rare, about 2 minutes per side. Remove from the heat and leave to rest on a warm plate.

5. Either serve on a platter or on individual plates, arranged as follows: the dressed salad should go on the bottom, then sprinkle over the corn and spring onions. Break (but don't crush) the tortilla chips over the top and sprinkle over the toasted pumpkin seeds. Slice the steak into thin pieces, cutting against the grain of the meat, and arrange on top of the salad. Spoon over the remaining dressing. Tuck in!

Spicy Prawn & Mango

This salad manages to be sour, salty, sweet, hot, crunchy, fresh all at the same time. It's a gorgeous, lively combination that we can't get enough of.

PREP TIME 10 MINUTES • COOK TIME 0 MINUTES

SoF / WF / GF / DF • SERVES 4 WITH OTHER DISHES

- 200g (7oz) mango, peeled and diced
- 200g (7oz) cucumber, diced
- 200g (7oz) cooked sustainable cold-water prawns, peeled
- 3 spring onions, finely chopped
- leaves from 2 sprigs of fresh mint, torn if large
- a big handful of fresh coriander leaves

FOR THE DRESSING:
- 3 tablespoons peanuts, roughly crushed
- 3 lime leaves, very finely chopped
- 1 tablespoon finely chopped hot red chilli
- 1 clove of garlic, crushed
- 1 tablespoon sugar
- 2 tablespoons fish sauce (check WF/GF, if needed)
- 1 tablespoon water

1. Place all the salad ingredients in a bowl.
2. Stir together the dressing ingredients, then spoon the dressing over the salad. Eat immediately.

TIP

Vegans and vegetarians can use vegan fish sauce and use sweetcorn in place of the prawns.

Spicy Miso-Roasted Chickpeas
with Cucumber & Radish

The mixture of miso and maple syrup lends these roasted chickpeas a sweet-savoury flavour that is just a bit addictive.

PREP TIME 15 MINUTES • COOK TIME 20 MINUTES

NF / WF / GF / DF / V / Ve • SERVES 4 WITH OTHER DISHES

- 2 × 400g (14oz) cans of chickpeas in water, drained
- 4 tablespoons vegetable or rapeseed oil
- 2 teaspoons maple syrup
- 1 tablespoon miso paste
- ½ teaspoon chilli powder, or to taste
- 100g (3½oz) radishes, chopped
- 150g (5½oz) cucumber, chopped
- 2 tablespoons finely chopped shallot (about 1 medium shallot)
- a big handful of flat-leaf parsley, finely chopped
- 1 tablespoon chilli oil (ready-made or see page 212 for Garlic & Chilli Oil)
- a pinch of salt
- 2 teaspoons pomegranate molasses, or more to taste

1. Heat the oven to 200°C fan/425°F/gas mark 7.
2. Place the chickpeas, oil, maple syrup, miso paste and chilli powder in a bowl and toss well so that each chickpea is coated (make sure the miso is well distributed and isn't forming a lump among the chickpeas). Tip onto a large baking tray (or 2 small ones), then roast in the oven for 20 minutes, or until crunchy.
3. Meanwhile, place the radishes, cucumber, shallot and parsley in another bowl. Add the chilli oil and a pinch of salt and toss.
4. When the chickpeas are ready, remove from the oven, cool slightly and add to the radish mixture. Spoon over the pomegranate molasses, toss again, and serve.

Warm Red Mullet
with Harissa & Couscous

Red mullet is a firm, sweet-fleshed fish, which makes it a good match for the warmth of the North African chilli paste, harissa. (In the UK, the most sustainable red mullet to choose is Cornish, at least 16cm/6¼in in size and not caught from May–July as this is when they spawn.)

PREP TIME 15 MINUTES • COOK TIME 18 MINUTES
SoF / NF / DF • SERVES 4

- 150g (5½oz) couscous
- 4 heaped teaspoons harissa paste
- 4 tablespoons extra-virgin olive oil, plus extra for the salad and for cooking
- 2 teaspoons freshly squeezed lemon juice
- ¼ red onion, very thinly sliced
- ½ head of fennel, very thinly sliced, plus any fronds
- 65g (2¼oz) cucumber, thinly sliced
- 2 big handfuls of rocket
- 1 orange, peel and pith sliced away, flesh chopped into small chunks (reserve any juice)
- a pinch of salt
- 8 red mullet fillets (or 4 whole mullet, if you prefer)

1. Cook the couscous according to the packet instructions (or pour over 150ml/5fl oz freshly boiled water, cover and leave to stand for 10 minutes). Drain, if necessary, and fluff up with a fork. Leave to cool slightly.
2. Stir together the harissa, oil and lemon juice.
3. Place the onion, fennel, cucumber, rocket, orange pieces and cooled couscous in a mixing bowl, add a splash of olive oil and a pinch of salt, and gently toss.
4. Place a wide frying pan over a high heat and add another splash of oil. Cook the fish fillets briskly, skin-side first, until slightly darkened and crispy looking, then turn and cook the other side – about 2 minutes per side (do this in batches, if necessary).
5. Divide the couscous salad among 4 plates and place the cooked fish on top. Spoon over the harissa dressing and any reserved orange juice. Eat warm.

Spiced Seafood
with Chilli, Lime & Corn

This is great on its own, but we wouldn't judge you if you loaded it up onto some just-fried corn tortillas to turn the salad into tacos or tostadas. (A squirt of the Chilli-lime Mayonnaise on page 79 wouldn't go amiss, or a sprinkle of crumbled feta – or do as we've done on page 166 and add a handful of tortilla chips.)

PREP TIME 10 MINUTES • COOK TIME 0 MINUTES

SoF / NF / WF / GF / DF • SERVES 4 WITH OTHER DISHES

- 300g (10½oz) cooked seafood mixture (or cold-water prawns, peeled and roughly chopped)
- 200g (7oz) cooked sweetcorn
- 1 tablespoon finely chopped hot red chilli
- 4 radishes, finely chopped
- 3 big handfuls of fresh coriander leaves
- 10 crisp lettuce leaves, chopped
- 6 tablespoons finely chopped pickled jalapeño peppers (hot or mild, to taste)
- 3 ripe plum tomatoes, deseeded and finely chopped
- ½ onion, very finely chopped
- freshly squeezed lime juice, to serve
- salt, to taste

1. Place all the salad ingredients in a bowl, squeeze over some lime juice and add a pinch of salt. Toss well and decide if it needs more seasoning, or even more chilli. Serve immediately.

Honeyed Harissa Roots & Grains

This is even prettier if you can find carrots in a variety of colours, or heritage varieties. We like to use a mixture of buckwheat and pearled spelt, which cook for the same length of time (or you can use 1½ ready-cooked mixed grain pouches), but you could also experiment with wheat-free options, like quinoa. If you want to make this more substantial, add feta, griddled halloumi or a handful of walnuts, pistachios or toasted flaked almonds. The Garlic Yoghurt on page 211 is really good here, too.

PREP TIME 15 MINUTES • COOK TIME 40 MINUTES

SoF / NF / V • SERVES 4

- 300g (10½oz) carrots (about 2 large), peeled and cut into 6 or 8 wedges
- 300g (10½oz) beetroot, peeled and cut into bite-sized chunks
- 2 tablespoons extra-virgin olive oil, plus extra for drizzling
- 1 tablespoon harissa paste
- 1 teaspoon honey
- 150g (5½oz) uncooked grains
- a big handful of mint leaves, roughly torn
- a big handful of flat-leaf parsley leaves, roughly torn
- 2 tablespoons finely chopped chives
- 1 tablespoon freshly squeezed lemon juice
- 4 tablespoons thick Greek-style yoghurt (or plant-based alternative)
- salt and freshly ground black pepper
- pomegranate molasses, to serve

1. Heat the oven to 200°C fan/425°F/gas mark 7.
2. Place the vegetables on a large baking tray. Stir together the olive oil, harissa, honey and a pinch of salt, then pour this mixture over the vegetables and use your hands to thoroughly coat each piece. Roast for 40 minutes, turning once halfway through, or until tender and slightly charred. Remove from the oven and allow to cool to warm or room temperature.
3. If using uncooked grains, cook according to the packet instructions. (If using buckwheat and pearled spelt, place in a pan of boiling salted water, cover and simmer for 20 minutes.) Drain, add a splash of oil, toss and then leave to cool.
4. When the grains are cool, add the herbs, lemon juice and some salt and pepper, and toss. Taste and adjust the seasoning, oil or lemon juice, if needed.
5. When ready to serve, divide the grains among 4 plates, then top with the roasted roots. At the very last minute, spoon over the yoghurt, then drizzle over a little pomegranate molasses.

Crab Cake & Mango

If your mango is really ripe and doesn't like being finely sliced, you can dice it and all the vegetables instead. As crab is expensive, we've kept portions of this one starter-sized.

PREP TIME 20 MINUTES • COOK TIME 18 MINUTES

SoF / NF • SERVES 4 AS A STARTER

FOR THE SALAD:
- 175g (6oz) cucumber, cut into ribbons
- 175g (6oz) mango, finely sliced
- 1 yellow pepper, very finely diced
- 2 spring onions, finely diced
- a handful of fresh coriander leaves
- 1 tablespoon finely chopped red chilli (or more, to taste)
- freshly squeezed lime juice, to taste
- a pinch of salt

FOR THE CHILLI-LIME MAYONNAISE:
- 2 tablespoons lime juice and a pinch of lime zest
- 4 heaped tablespoons mayonnaise
- a generous pinch of hot chilli powder

FOR THE CRAB CAKES:
- 300g (10½oz) crab meat, both brown and white
- 2 spring onions, finely chopped
- 1 tablespoon finely chopped red chilli
- 1 tablespoon lime juice
- 6 lime leaves, ribs removed, very finely chopped
- 75g (2½oz) panko breadcrumbs
- salt and freshly ground black pepper
- 2 eggs, beaten
- oil, for cooking

1. Place all the salad ingredients in a bowl, seasoning with the juice of half a lime and a little pinch of salt at first. Taste and adjust if needed – it should be sweet-sour.

2. Stir together the chilli-lime mayonnaise ingredients in a separate bowl.

3. In a large bowl, mix together all the crab cake ingredients, except the cooking oil.

4. Heat a 5mm (¼in) depth of oil in a wide frying pan over a medium heat. Working in batches, scoop small tablespoon-sized balls of the crab mixture and place in the hot oil, pressing down to flatten slightly. Cook the crab cakes until golden brown on the bottom, 3–4 minutes depending on your pan, then turn and cook the other sides. Remove to a plate lined with kitchen paper or a clean tea towel while you cook the rest – you should be able to make about 20 crab cakes. Keep warm.

5. Divide the mango salad among 4 plates and top with the crab cakes. Serve with a dollop of the mayo on the side.

Griddled Hispi & Crispy Tofu
with Sweet Soy Dressing

If you don't find yourself feverishly dipping the crunchy crumbs of tofu into the dressing...well, you aren't as greedy as us. If you want an alternative to tofu, chopped roasted peanuts work well.

PREP TIME 20 MINUTES • COOK TIME 15 MINUTES

NF / WF / GF / DF / V / Ve • SERVES 4

- 200g (7oz) extra-firm tofu, crumbled into small pieces
- 6 tablespoons cornflour
- oil, for cooking
- 3 cloves of garlic, very finely sliced (optional)
- 1 head of hispi or sweetheart cabbage, cut into 8 wedges
- 2 spring onions, finely sliced on an angle
- 2 red chillies, finely sliced on an angle

FOR THE DRESSING:

- 4 tablespoons tamari or soy sauce (check WF/GF, if needed)
- 6 tablespoons water
- 1 tablespoon sugar
- 2 teaspoons cornflour

→ *Pictured overleaf*

1. For the dressing, place the tamari, water and sugar in a small saucepan and bring to a simmer. Place the cornflour in a small bowl and add 2 tablespoons of the hot tamari mixture. Whisk until smooth, then gradually pour it back into pan, stirring continuously. Cook for another few minutes, stirring constantly, until thickened and glossy. Taste – you shouldn't be able to detect any chalkiness from the cornflour. Set aside.

2. Tip the tofu into a bowl, add the cornflour and toss gently until each piece is well covered.

3. Heat a 5mm (¼in) depth of oil in a wide frying pan over a medium heat. When hot, add the tofu and spread it out. Cook, stirring now and then, until crisp and golden, about 5–6 minutes. If the pieces stick together, gently break them up. Remove from the pan with a slotted spoon and set aside.

4. Add the garlic to the same pan and cook until it begins to turn golden, then immediately remove from the pan with the slotted spoon. If left to go deep gold, it will taste bitter.

5. Set a clean wide frying pan over a medium heat, add a splash of oil and, when hot, add the hispi, cut-sides down. Cook for 2–3 minutes, until the cut edges begin to darken and char, then turn each piece and char the other cut sides.

6. Arrange the hispi pieces on a serving platter, sprinkle over the crisp tofu, then spoon over the sweet soy dressing. Garnish with the fried garlic, spring onions and red chillies. Eat warm.

Spiced Crispy Duck
with Watermelon

Sweet watermelon, crispy spiced duck, chilli heat and sour lime –
this is a showstopping combination.

PREP TIME 20 MINUTES • COOK TIME 1½ HOURS

SoF / NF / WF / GF / DF • SERVES 4

- 1 teaspoon Szechuan peppercorns
- 1 teaspoon fennel seeds
- ½ teaspoon ground cinnamon
- ½ teaspoon ground ginger
- 1 teaspoon flaky sea salt (or ½ teaspoon fine salt)
- 4 duck legs (see tip)

FOR THE SALAD:
- 500g (1lb 2oz) watermelon, cubed
- 2 big handfuls of coriander leaves
- 4 spring onions, halved lengthways and sliced on an angle
- 400g (14oz) cucumber, diced
- 1 red chilli, deseeded and finely sliced
- leaves from 3 bushy sprigs of mint

FOR THE DRESSING:
- 1 tablespoon lime juice, plus extra to serve
- 2 teaspoons fish sauce, plus extra if needed

1. Heat the oven to 180°C fan/400°F/gas mark 6.
2. Place the peppercorns, fennel seeds, cinnamon, ginger and salt in a pestle and mortar or spice grinder and grind until sandy in texture.
3. Prick the duck legs all over with a pin or the tip of a sharp knife – this helps the fat render out and the skin to crisp up. Rub the spice mix all over each leg, then place them on a rack set inside a baking dish. Roast for 1½ hours, basting once after an hour. When done, the skin will be crisp and crunchy looking. Remove the legs from the oven and set aside, allowing to cool slightly and rest for a few minutes.
4. Place the salad ingredients in a mixing bowl, add the lime juice and fish sauce and toss. Taste and add another teaspoon of fish sauce if it needs more salty savouriness.
5. Pull the warm duck meat and crispy skin from the bones and break the meat into bite-sized pieces. Divide the salad among wide bowls, arrange the duck meat on top, squeeze over a little more lime juice and eat while the duck is still warm.

→ *Pictured overleaf*

TIP

Duck legs can vary in size from 220g (8oz) to 350g (12oz), or even 400g (14oz), so judge how many you need by their size, while also remembering that the fat will render out, so they shrink a little once cooked.

1

Coconut Moong Dhal
with Turmeric Spiced Fish

Koshambari is a salad made with split yellow mung dal, and we included a recipe for it in our book, 'Happy Curries', a few years back. It is absolutely perfect with gently spiced white fish.

PREP TIME 15 MINUTES • COOK TIME 38 MINUTES

SoF / WF / GF / DF • SERVES 4

FOR THE SALAD:
- 125g (4½oz) yellow mung/moong dal
- 2 tablespoons neutral oil
- 1½ tablespoons mustard seeds
- 10 curry leaves, roughly torn
- 4 tablespoons desiccated coconut
- 100g (3½oz) peanuts or cashews, chopped into small pieces (optional)
- 200g (7oz) cucumber, finely diced
- a large handful of coriander leaves, roughly chopped
- freshly squeezed lemon juice
- a pinch of salt

FOR THE DRESSING:
- 4 heaped tablespoons coconut cream from the top of an unshaken can
- 1 tablespoon freshly squeezed lemon juice
- ½ teaspoon ground turmeric
- 2 teaspoons finely chopped red chilli
- a pinch of salt

FOR THE FISH:
- 2 tablespoons chickpea (gram) flour
- 1 teaspoon ground turmeric
- ½ teaspoon ground coriander
- ½ teaspoon chilli powder
- salt and freshly ground black pepper
- 4 sustainable white fish fillets
- neutral oil, for cooking

1. Rinse the yellow dal under cold running water. Place in a pan and cover with fresh cold water, bring to a rolling boil, then reduce to a simmer for 30 minutes until tender, but not falling apart, skimming off any foam or scum that rises to the top.

2. Meanwhile, set a small frying pan over a medium heat. Add the oil and the mustard seeds. When they start to pop, remove a teaspoonful of the mustard seeds and oil, and set aside (for the dressing). Add the curry leaves, coconut and nuts to the pan and cook, stirring constantly, for 2–3 minutes, until just golden brown – be sure not to burn them. Remove from the heat and tip this mixture straight into a salad bowl.

3. Drain the dal, then cool under cold running water. Add them to the bowl along with the cucumber, coriander leaves and a little squeeze of lemon. Add a small pinch of salt, then toss and taste, adding more salt or lemon as needed.

4. Make the dressing: stir all the ingredients together, including the reserved mustard seeds.

5. For the fish, mix together the flour, spices and seasoning, then dredge the fish in this mixture, turning to coat well.

6. Place a frying pan over a medium heat, add a splash of oil, then cook the fish for 2–4 minutes per side, depending on the thickness of each fillet, until just cooked through.

7. Divide the dal salad among plates, top with the fish and serve with the coconut dressing on the side.

Lemongrass & Chilli Beef

This is inspired by a Vietnamese salad called goi bo, but our version is quite different – the true version often uses raw beef. You could add a clove of garlic to the dressing for even more oomph.

PREP TIME 15 MINUTES • **COOK TIME 6 MINUTES PLUS RESTING**

SoF / WF / GF / DF • **SERVES 4**

- 80g (3oz) cucumber, very finely sliced
- 8 crisp lettuce leaves, chopped or torn
- a large handful of coriander leaves
- leaves from 4 bushy sprigs of mint, torn if large
- a handful of watercress
- 1 medium carrot, julienned into fine matchsticks
- 1 shallot, finely sliced
- 3 tablespoons chopped roasted unsalted peanuts
- crispy onions (from a packet), to serve

FOR THE DRESSING:
- 1 stick of lemongrass, tough outer removed and discarded, very finely chopped
- 1½ tablespoons fish sauce (check WF/GF, if needed)
- 1½ tablespoon lime juice
- 2 lime leaves, ribs removed, very, very finely chopped
- 2 teaspoons caster sugar
- 1 hot red chilli, finely chopped
- 3 tablespoons water

FOR THE STEAK:
- vegetable oil, for cooking
- 600g (1lb 5oz) sirloin steak, fat trimmed away

1. Place all the salad ingredients, except the crispy onions, in a bowl and toss.
2. Stir together the dressing ingredients in a separate bowl.
3. Place a frying pan over a high heat. When the pan is really hot, add a splash of oil. Place the steak into the pan and sear – the aim is to create a flavourful deep brown exterior on the meat, while keeping the interior rare. Cook for 2–3 minutes, depending on the thickness of the meat, then turn and repeat. The meat will feel very soft when pressed if the inside is rare, but will firm up as it cooks more. Remove the steak from the pan and leave to rest for 5 minutes or so.
4. Slice the steak into thin strips about 5mm (¼in) thick.
5. Spoon half of the dressing into the salad bowl (being sure to catch the red chilli and lemongrass pieces) and toss, then add the steak and toss again. Serve the salad with the remaining dressing on the side, and finish each portion with a pinch of crispy onions.

→ *Pictured overleaf*

Thai Basil Prawns & Noodles

This is distantly related to yum woon sen – a glass noodle salad that Rebecca sometimes chooses in Thai restaurants, often made with minced pork as well as seafood, and Thai celery, which is leafier than European celery. To make it a slightly closer relative, try making this with glass noodles.

PREP TIME 15 MINUTES • COOK TIME 12 MINUTES
SoF / WF / GF / DF • SERVES 4

- 300g (10½oz) rice stick noodles
- a splash of vegetable or rapeseed oil
- 100g (3½oz) sustainable cold-water prawns, raw and fresh, or cooked and frozen
- ½ small red onion, finely sliced
- 2 sticks of celery, finely sliced, and any leaves roughly chopped
- 100g (3½oz) cherry tomatoes, chopped
- 75g (2½oz) roasted peanuts, roughly chopped
- 12 Thai basil leaves, roughly torn

FOR THE DRESSING:
- 2 tablespoons finely chopped red chilli
- 2 tablespoons freshly squeezed lime juice
- 1 tablespoon fish sauce (check WF/GF, if needed), or to taste
- 2 tablespoons water
- ½ teaspoon sugar

1. Cook the rice stick noodles according to the packet instructions. Drain and set aside to cool.
2. Stir all the dressing ingredients together in a small bowl until the sugar has completely dissolved. Taste and add more fish sauce if needed – it should be really punchy.
3. Set a small frying pan over a medium heat and add a splash of oil. Add the prawns and sauté for about 2 minutes until cooked through and piping hot.
4. Combine the onion, celery, tomatoes, peanuts and basil leaves in a bowl, along with the noodles and cooked prawns. Pour the dressing into the bowl and toss the salad. Divide among serving bowls and eat immediately.

⟶ *Pictured overleaf*

TIP

If you have leftover Thai basil which might go to waste, freeze it in sprigs to use later in Thai curries.

1. Thai Basil Prawns &
   Noodles *page 87*
2. Lemongrass &
   Chilli Beef *page 86*

Thai-Style Crispy Rice & Spicy Sausage

in Lettuce Cups

This is very (very) loosely based on the flavours found in a salad from Laos, called nam khao (yam naem in Thailand). In our version, rice is fried until crisp with curry paste and air-dried sausage, then mixed with herbs, ginger and spring onions and eaten rolled up in lettuce leaves. If you can't find the right kind of sausage, you could use any fairly plain air-dried salami instead.

PREP TIME 10 MINUTES • COOK TIME 25 MINUTES

SoF / WF / GF / DF • SERVES 4

- 100g (3½oz) uncooked jasmine rice
- vegetable oil, for cooking
- 300g (10½oz) semi-dried Thai or Chinese sausage, cut into small pieces (check WF/GF/SoF, if needed)
- 1 heaped tablespoon good-quality Thai red curry paste (try to find a Thai brand, if you can)
- ½ red onion, finely sliced
- a big handful of coriander leaves
- leaves from 2 bushy sprigs of mint, torn if large
- 2 spring onions, finely chopped
- 4cm (1½in) piece of fresh ginger, finely sliced into matchsticks
- 2 teaspoons fish sauce (check WF/GF, if needed)
- juice of 1 lime
- 8–12 soft lettuce leaves, depending on their size
- 4 tablespoons roasted peanuts, chopped

1. Wash the rice in two changes of water, then place in a small pan with a lid. Add enough cold water to cover, bring to a simmer, cover with the lid and cook for about 12 minutes, or until the rice is tender. Tip out onto a plate (you shouldn't need to drain it) and leave to steam dry for a few minutes.

2. Add a splash of oil to a wide frying pan set over a medium heat and add the sausage pieces. Sauté, turning often, until golden and crisp. Remove from the pan and keep warm.

3. Add the red curry paste to the rice and mix until each grain is coated. Return the pan (and its sausage fat) to the heat and add the rice mixture. Cook, stirring now and then, until parts of the rice begin to turn golden and crisp.

4. Meanwhile, place the onion, coriander, mint, spring onions, ginger, fish sauce and lime juice in a bowl. Toss, then add the partially crispy, hot and spicy rice to the bowl, along with the sausage, and toss again. Taste: it should be sour and slightly salty, with a pleasing level of chilli heat from the curry paste.

5. Arrange 2–3 lettuce leaves on 4 serving plates, depending on how large the leaves are, then spoon the salad onto the leaves. Top with the peanuts and eat by rolling the lettuce leaves around the spiced crunchy rice salad.

Salt & Szechuan Pepper Tofu
with Cabbage & Ginger Salad

*Crispy tofu spiced with lip-tingling Szechuan pepper and chilli,
on a crunchy cabbage and ginger salad. Yes please.*

PREP TIME 15 MINUTES • COOK TIME 10–12 MINUTES

NF / WF / GF / DF / V / Ve • SERVES 4

FOR THE TOFU:

- 2 teaspoons Szechuan peppercorns
- 2 star anise
- 1 teaspoon fennel seeds
- 1 teaspoon sesame seeds
- ¼ teaspoon ground cinnamon
- ½ teaspoon fine salt
- 8 twists of freshly ground black pepper
- 1 teaspoon soft brown sugar
- 4 heaped tablespoons cornflour
- 400g (14oz) extra-firm tofu, patted dry and cut into 2cm (¾in) pieces
- vegetable or rapeseed oil, for cooking
- ½ red onion, finely chopped
- ½ red chilli, finely sliced
- 2 cloves of garlic, finely chopped

FOR THE SALAD:

- ½ red chilli, finely chopped
- 200g (7oz) cucumber, diced
- 4cm (1½in) piece of fresh ginger, peeled and sliced into thin matchsticks
- 2 spring onions, finely chopped
- 100g (3½oz) white cabbage, finely shredded
- 2 teaspoons tamari (check WF/GF, if needed)
- 2 teaspoons sesame oil
- juice of ½ lime, or to taste, plus 4 wedges to serve

1. Place all the tofu spices, salt, pepper and sugar in a pestle and mortar or spice grinder and grind to a fine powder.

2. Mix about 6 teaspoons of the spice mixture (reserving what's left) with the cornflour in a large mixing bowl. Add the tofu pieces and gently toss, using your hands, until each piece is well dusted.

3. Heat a 5mm (¼in) depth of oil in a wide frying pan over a medium heat. Add the tofu pieces and fry until each piece is golden on one side, then turn and cook on all sides, a total of 8–10 minutes. Remove with a slotted spoon to drain on a plate lined with kitchen paper or a clean tea towel.

4. Keep the pan on the heat and add the onion, sliced chilli and garlic. Fry briefly for about 2 minutes, being careful not to burn the garlic, until the onion is just beginning to soften. Remove with a slotted spoon to the plate with the tofu.

5. To make the salad place the chopped raw chilli, cucumber, ginger, spring onions and cabbage in a serving bowl, add the tamari, sesame oil and lime juice, then toss.

6. Serve the salad topped with the crisp tofu and fried vegetables, sprinkling over a pinch of the reserved spice mix just before eating. Leave extra tamari soy sauce, spice mix and lime wedges on the table for guests to help themselves.

Chorizo
with Grains & Green Beans

We usually advocate cooking grains from scratch rather than buying ready-cooked (it's cheaper), but every now and then we all need a very fast, very tasty meal. So, here you go. The chorizo lends this dish plenty of flavour, so it doesn't really warrant a dressing, but a little smoked paprika mayo makes it feel extra indulgent (2 tablespoons of mayonnaise plus 2 tablespoons of water, or enough to thin so you can pour it, and a big pinch of smoked paprika).

PREP TIME 10 MINUTES • COOK TIME 12 MINUTES

SoF / NF / DF • SERVES 4

- 350g (12oz) cooking chorizo, roughly chopped
- 100g (3½oz) green beans, trimmed and sliced into 3–4cm (1–1½in) pieces – blanch and refresh
- 2 × 250g (9oz) pouches of ready-cooked mixed grains and/or pulses (Spanish-style work well) (check DF/NF/SoF, if needed)
- 1 small red onion, very finely sliced
- a large handful of rocket
- a large handful of coriander leaves, roughly chopped
- a large handful of flat-leaf parsley, roughly chopped
- extra-virgin olive oil, to serve
- freshly squeezed lemon juice, to serve

1. Place a wide frying pan over a medium heat. When hot, add the chorizo (don't add any oil as it contains plenty) and cook, stirring and turning, until each piece is golden brown.

2. Blanch the beans in a small pan of boiling water for 3 minutes. Drain and set aside.

3. Warm the grains according the packet instructions. Allow to cool a little, then place in a bowl and toss together with the green beans, red onion, rocket, coriander, parsley and cooked chorizo.

4. Serve on a platter or individual plates, with a little olive oil spooned over the top and a squeeze of lemon (you probably won't need to season with any salt as chorizo is very salty).

TIP

If you've got a bit more time and energy, the Jammy Eggs on page 44 are great with this, as are the Roasted Chickpeas on page 105.

Warm Gochujang Short Ribs
with Rice Noodle Salad

If you only make one recipe from this book (and you eat meat) – make it this one.

PREP TIME 20 MINUTES • COOK TIME UP TO 3 HOURS

NF / DF • SERVES 4

- 150g (5½oz) dried rice vermicelli noodles, cooked according to packet instructions and tossed together with 1 teaspoon sesame oil
- a big handful of coriander leaves
- leaves from 2 bushy sprigs of mint, torn
- 100g (3½oz) cucumber, in matchsticks
- 2 tablespoons finely chopped shallot (about 1 small shallot)
- 3 radishes, finely sliced
- ½ stick of lemongrass, tougher outer removed and discarded, finely chopped
- 10 romaine lettuce leaves, chopped

  2 tablespoons each of lime juice, sesame oil, fish sauce and chopped kimchi

FOR THE SHORT RIBS:
- a splash of vegetable oil
- 4 beef short ribs, on the bone (at least 1.2 kg/2lb 10oz)
- 2½ tablespoons tamari (check WF/GF, if needed)
- 2½ tablespoons each mirin and sesame oil
- 4 heaped tablespoons gochujang paste
- 7 cloves of garlic, crushed
- 4cm (1½in) fresh ginger, peeled and grated
- 1 onion, halved and finely sliced
- up to 500ml (18fl oz) hot beef, chicken or vegetable stock

1. For the ribs, heat the oven to 170°C fan/375°F/gas mark 5. Heat the oil in an ovenproof pan with a tight-fitting lid over a medium heat. Add the ribs and brown all over, then remove from the heat and arrange so the bones face down in the pan.

2. Stir together the tamari, mirin, sesame oil, gochujang, garlic and ginger, then spoon over the meat. Add the onion and pour 300ml (10fl oz) of the stock around the ribs, without washing off the sauce. Add the lid and place in the oven for 2½ hours, basting with the sauce after 1½ hours and adding 100ml (3½fl oz) stock if needed (the sauce should be reduced and sticky by now). Cover again and return to the oven for the final hour until the meat is shreddable (if it's not, return to the oven for 30 minutes with another splash of stock). Set aside until cool enough to handle, then transfer the meat to a plate.

3. Discard the excess oil from inside the pan, keeping 1 tablespoonful aside, leaving the sticky-sweet sauce and soft onions. Pull the meat from the bones and shred into pieces. Return the meat to the pan and discard the bones. (If the meat and sauce are now cold, warm gently over a low heat.)

4. Add the remaining ingredients, apart from the kimchi, to the cooked noodles. Add the reserved spiced oil from the pan and toss. Divide among 4 plates, top with the shredded beef and spoon over some of the sticky sauce from the pan. Serve the chopped kimchi in a little bowl on the table so your guests can decide if they want to try it – its hot sourness cuts brilliantly through the rich, sweet, spicy beef.

Spiced Lentils

with Crispy Rotis & Garlic Yoghurt

Quick enough to make for a weekday lunch; pretty enough to serve to friends at the weekend. If you have any chaat masala (a sour spice mix) in the cupboard, a pinch on top is very welcome here.

PREP TIME 15 MINUTES • COOK TIME 22 MINUTES

SoF / NF / V • SERVES 4

- vegetable or rapeseed oil, for cooking
- 1 onion, halved and finely sliced
- 2 × 400g (14oz) cans of cooked lentils (ideally green), drained
- 1 teaspoon chilli flakes
- 1 teaspoon garam masala
- 1 teaspoon ground turmeric
- a pinch of salt
- freshly squeezed lemon juice

FOR THE SALAD:
- 2 roti flatbreads, halved and cut into triangles
- 2 big handfuls of rocket or watercress
- a big handful of coriander leaves
- 120g (4oz) fennel, finely diced, any fronds reserved and chopped
- leaves from 2 bushy sprigs of mint, torn if large
- 3 tablespoons finely chopped chives
- 1 tablespoon finely chopped red chilli
- Garlic Yoghurt (see page 211)

FOR THE TEMPER:
- 1 teaspoon mustard seeds
- 8 curry leaves, torn

1. Heat a splash of oil in a wide frying pan over a medium heat. When hot, add the onion and sauté, stirring often, until beginning to brown, 8–10 minutes. Add the drained lentils, chilli flakes, garam masala and turmeric and cook, stirring often, until the onions are soft and the spices are fragrant. Remove from the heat, season with a pinch of salt and a squeeze of lemon, and keep warm.

2. Wipe out the frying pan (or use a fresh one), set over a medium heat and pour in a 5mm (¼in) depth of vegetable oil. When hot (but not smoking hot), add the roti triangles and fry until golden, turning once. Don't let them get too dark or they will taste bitter. Remove with tongs or a slotted spoon to drain on a plate lined with kitchen paper or a clean tea towel.

3. Carefully spoon most of the oil out of the frying pan (you can save it to use again) and return it to the heat to make the temper. Add the mustard seeds and curry leaves, and cook until the mustard seeds pop and crackle. Remove from the heat.

4. Serve on a large platter or on individual plates. Arrange the rocket or watercress, coriander and fennel on the bottom, spoon over the spiced lentils, then arrange the fried roti on top. Spoon over the yoghurt, sprinkle over the remaining herbs and the chopped chilli, then drizzle the temper on top, being careful not to make the salad oily. Eat immediately.

'Nduja

with Semi-dried Tomatoes, Chickpeas, Spelt & Rocket

'Nduja is a powerhouse of an ingredient: a spreadable and fairly spicy salami from Calabria in Italy. It's used in all sorts of ways (so don't worry if you have some left over – it will keep for several weeks in the fridge), often with mozzarella or burrata, chickpeas or spelt. Spelt, an ancient form of wheat, is called farro in Italy. Spelt grains or pearled spelt tend to cook a bit quicker than proper Italian farro, which may need an overnight soak and about twice the cooking time. Make sure everything is at room temperature before assembling.

PREP TIME 15 MINUTES • COOKING TIME 20 MINUTES

SoF / NF • SERVES 4

- 100g (3½oz) spelt grains or pearled spelt, rinsed
- 2 big handfuls of rocket
- 1½ × 400g (14oz) tins of chickpeas, drained (save the remaining chickpeas for another salad)
- 1 tablespoon lemon juice
- 1 tablespoon extra-virgin olive oil, plus extra to serve
- 200g (7oz) semi-dried or sun-blush tomatoes, roughly chopped
- 35g (1¼oz) 'nduja, broken into little pieces
- 2 × 125g (4½oz) balls of buffalo mozzarella, torn into chunks
- salt

1. Simmer the spelt in boiling salted water for 20 minutes, or cook according to the packet instructions, until tender. Drain and then spread out on a plate to cool.

2. Toss together the spelt, rocket, chickpeas, lemon juice, olive oil and a pinch of salt. Tip onto a serving platter or onto individual plates, then dot the top of the salad with the semi-dried tomatoes, 'nduja and mozzarella pieces. Drizzle over a little more olive oil before tucking in.

3

GOOD
&
HEARTY

Roast & Raw Cauliflower, Chickpeas, Fennel & Herbs

The idea of mixing both raw and roast cauliflower came to us via the Ottolenghi book, 'Simple' – it makes for a really clever mixture of textures of flavours. We love this as it is, or topped with fried or griddled halloumi, crumbled feta or leftover roast chicken.

PREP TIME 15 MINUTES • COOK TIME 30 MINUTES

SoF / WF / GF / DF / V / Ve • SERVES 4

- 1 medium cauliflower, about 800g (1lb 12oz), and its leaves, divided into thirds
- 150g (5½oz) shallots, trimmed and cut into 1cm (½in) wedges
- salt and freshly ground black pepper
- 2 tablespoons olive oil
- 40g (1½oz) flaked almonds
- 3 tablespoons finely chopped flat-leaf parsley
- 2 tablespoons finely chopped dill
- ½ head of fennel, trimmed and finely diced
- 70g (2½oz) cucumber, finely diced
- 1 teaspoon ground cumin, or to taste
- 1 tablespoon lemon juice
- a drizzle of good-quality extra-virgin olive oil

FOR THE ROASTED CHICKPEAS:
- 1 × 400g (14oz) cans of chickpeas, drained
- ½ teaspoon ground cumin
- ½ teaspoon ground coriander
- ½ teaspoon smoked paprika
- salt and freshly ground black pepper
- 1 tablespoon olive oil

1. Heat the oven to 200°C fan/425°F/gas mark 7.
2. Break two thirds of the cauliflower into small florets and roughly chop the leaves. Arrange in a single layer on a large baking tray with the shallots. Season with salt and pepper, drizzle over the oil and toss to coat. Cook in the oven for 15 minutes, then add the almonds, toss again and cook for a further 5 minutes until the florets and leaves are beginning to char, the shallot is soft and the almonds golden. If the leaves char much quicker, remove them from the tray and set aside.
3. Meanwhile, tip the chickpeas onto a clean tea towel. Fold the tea towel over, enclosing the chickpeas, and rub back and forth to remove the skins. Pick out the skinned chickpeas and place on another baking tray. Add the chickpea spices, salt, pepper and olive oil and toss thoroughly. Roast in the oven for 20 minutes until crunchy, then remove from the oven and leave to cool for 5 minutes.
4. Coarsely grate the remaining cauliflower into a bowl. Add the parsley, dill, fennel and cucumber, then add the contents of both trays (and the cooked leaves) to the bowl, along with the cumin, lemon juice and a little drizzle of extra-virgin olive oil. Toss really well and taste, adding more salt or cumin, as needed. Serve immediately.

Beetroot Fritters

with Feta & Spinach Yoghurt

If you're used to northern European salads, this may surprise you – there's almost nothing raw here. But in many countries, cooked vegetables served at room temperature are considered salads The base for this one is inspired by a Turkish salad, yoğurtlu ıspanak salatası.

PREP TIME 25 MINUTES • COOK TIME 20 MINUTES

SoF / WF / GF / V • SERVES 4

- neutral oil, for cooking
- 1 teaspoon mustard seeds
- 1 teaspoon cumin seeds
- 1 teaspoon nigella seeds
- 150g (5½oz) chickpea (gram) flour
- 40g (1½oz) rice flour
- ½ teaspoon baking powder
- 700g (1lb 9oz) raw beetroot (about 4 medium), peeled and cut into matchsticks
- 1 onion, finely sliced
- 1 green chilli, deseeded and finely chopped
- 1 tablespoon lime juice
- up to 150ml (5fl oz) cold water
- salt and freshly ground black pepper

FOR THE SALAD:
- 300g (10½oz) frozen whole leaf spinach, cooked and squeezed of excess liquid
- 500g (1lb 2oz) thick Greek yoghurt
- 1 clove of garlic, crushed to a paste (for a milder flavour, blanch in boiling water)
- 2 spring onions, halved lengthways and finely chopped (optional)
- 3 tablespoons finely chopped fresh mint
- a pinch of salt
- 150g (5½oz) feta cheese, crumbled
- a handful of roughly chopped walnuts
- leaves from 4 bushy sprigs of dill

1. Place a small frying pan over a medium heat with a splash of oil. Add the mustard seeds and when they start to pop, add the cumin seeds. Cook for 30 seconds, then scrape into a large mixing bowl. Add the nigella seeds, chickpea flour, rice flour, baking powder, a generous pinch of salt and lots of pepper. Mix well. Add the beetroot, onion, green chilli, lime juice and about 5 tablespoons of water. Continue very gradually adding water, up to a maximum of 150ml (5fl oz), and mixing until a loose (bright pink!) batter forms, incorporating all the dry ingredients. It will look very wet – don't worry.

2. Set a deep saucepan over a medium heat and add a 6cm (2½in) depth of cooking oil. Heat the oil so that a cube of bread fizzes and browns in 30 seconds. Turn the oven onto the lowest heat. Line a plate with a clean tea towel.

3. Use kitchen tongs to grab a 2cm (¾in) bundle of the beetroot mixture and gently place it in the oil. Work in batches and don't overcrowd the pan. Fry until crisp all over, 1–2 minutes, then remove from the oil to drain on the lined plate. Keep warm in the oven. Continue with the rest of the mixture.

4. Tip the spinach, yoghurt, garlic, spring onions, if using, mint and salt into another bowl, and stir well. Taste for seasoning.

5. Thickly spread the spinach yoghurt over 4 plates. Top with the fritters, scatter over the feta and the walnut pieces, finish with fresh dill and eat immediately.

LEON Rainbow Salad

with Harissa

This is another at-home version of one of our most popular restaurant salads.
(If you prefer it with smoked garlic aioli rather than harissa, see page 215 and swap
the fresh garlic for smoked garlic or smoked garlic paste in a jar).

PREP TIME 20 MINUTES • COOK TIME 40 MINUTES

SoF / NF / WF / GF / DF / V / Ve • SERVES 4

- 1 red onion, cut into 2cm (¾in) wedges
- 250g (9oz) celeriac, cut into 2cm (¾in) chunks
- 350g (12oz) butternut squash, cut into 2cm (¾in) chunks
- 150g (5½oz) carrot, cut into 2cm (¾in) chunks
- 1 teaspoon nigella seeds
- 1 teaspoon ground turmeric
- 2 tablespoons olive oil
- salt and freshly ground black pepper
- 1 × 400g (14oz) can of chickpeas, drained
- 2 big handfuls of baby spinach
- 2 big handfuls of rocket
- 1 tablespoon diced Pink Pickled Onions (homemade, page 217, or from a jar, or use sauerkraut)
- 50g (1¾oz) pickled red peppers (or roasted peppers from a jar), drained and sliced

FOR THE DRESSING:

- 4 tablespoons good-quality vegan mayonnaise (check SoF/NF, if needed)
- 2 teaspoons harissa paste, or to taste
- 2 teaspoons freshly squeezed lemon juice, or to taste
- water, to thin

1. Heat the oven to 200°C fan/425°F/gas mark 7.
2. Tip the onion, celeriac, squash and carrot onto a baking tray. Add the nigella seeds, turmeric, 1 tablespoon of the oil and lots of salt and pepper. Use a spoon to toss until everything is coated (you can use your hands, but they will turn yellow!). Place in the oven and set a timer for 20 minutes.
3. Tip the chickpeas onto a clean tea towel, fold it over to enclose them and rub back and forth to remove the skins. Pick out the skinned chickpeas and place on another baking tray, with some salt and pepper and another tablespoon of olive oil and toss thoroughly to coat. When the timer goes off, add the tray to the oven and roast alongside the vegetables (turn them at this point, too) for 20 minutes, or until crunchy. Remove both trays from the oven and leave to cool until just warm.
4. Stir together the mayo and harissa for the dressing and squeeze in the lemon juice. Add just enough water – a splash – to thin the dressing until it's pourable. Taste and add more harissa or lemon, if needed.
5. Divide the spinach and rocket among 4 plates or wide shallow bowls, then add the vegetables and the crunchy roasted chickpeas. Scatter over the pickled onions (or sauerkraut) and pickled or roasted peppers, then spoon over the dressing and a final pinch of salt. Eat while warm.

Artichoke & Sautéed Potato

with Anchovy & Caper Dressing

As with many of our artichoke recipes, the trick here is to get really good quality grilled artichokes.

PREP TIME 15 MINUTES • COOK TIME 20 MINUTES

SoF / NF / WF / GF / DF • SERVES 4 WITH OTHER DISHES

- 500g (1lb 2oz) new potatoes (or charlotte or baby potatoes), halved or quartered if large
- oil, for cooking
- 150g (5½oz) grilled artichokes in oil, from a jar (not canned), drained well and chopped into 2–3cm (¾–1¼in) pieces
- a small bunch of flat-leaf parsley leaves, chopped if very large
- Anchovy & Caper Dressing (see page 214)
- salt

1. Cook the potatoes in a pan of boiling salted water until tender, about 12 minutes, then drain.
2. Place a frying pan over a medium heat and add a splash of cooking oil. Sauté the potatoes, turning often, until golden all over. Remove from the heat, draining the oil back into the pan, and leave to cool a little. They should be warm, but not hot, when added to the salad.
3. Place the sautéed potatoes in a mixing bowl and add the artichokes and parsley. Spoon over half of the dressing and toss well. Taste, adding more of the dressing as needed (but be careful not to make the dish oily). Serve at room temperature.

TIP

If artichokes aren't your thing, the potatoes and dressing are good with wedges of soft-boiled egg or griddled asparagus spears.

Puy Lentils

with Roast Tomatoes, Smoky Aubergine & Fried Eggs

Rebecca really loves the Turkish breakfast dish, cilbir, with eggs, yoghurt and butter melted together with Turkish red pepper flakes. We've used similar flavours here, along with Puy lentils, sweet roasted tomatoes, smoky aubergine and the crunch of toasted walnuts. The lentil, roasted tomato and herb mixture is delicious on its own, and also works as a side.

PREP TIME 15 MINUTES • COOK TIME 30 MINUTES

SoF / WF / GF / V • SERVES 4

- 1 aubergine, halved
- 200g (7oz) cherry tomatoes
- 200g (7oz) shallots, cut into 1cm (½in) wedges
- 2 tablespoons extra-virgin olive oil
- 80g (3oz) walnuts, roughly chopped
- 200g (7oz) Puy lentils
- 1 clove of garlic, crushed
- 1½ tablespoons freshly squeezed lemon juice
- a small bunch of flat-leaf parsley leaves, finely chopped
- a generous pinch of salt
- 40g (1½oz) butter (or plant-based alternative)
- 2 teaspoons paprika
- a pinch of red chilli flakes or red pepper flakes, to taste
- neutral oil, for cooking
- 4 eggs
- 4 tablespoons thick Greek-style yoghurt (or use your favourite plant-based alternative)

1. Heat the grill to its highest setting, and cook the aubergine until the skin is blistered all over (or use a gas ring). Place in a bowl to cool.
2. Heat the oven to 200°C fan/425°F/gas mark 7.
3. Place the tomatoes and shallots on a baking tray, add the oil and toss to coat. Roast for 15 minutes, then add the walnuts and cook for 5 minutes more. The tomatoes should be collapsing and the shallots soft and beginning to char.
4. Place the lentils in a pan of water and bring to a simmer. Cook for 20 minutes, until tender. Drain and tip into a bowl. When cooled slightly, add the garlic, lemon juice, parsley, salt and the cooked shallots, tomatoes and walnuts. Toss gently. Tip the mixture onto a large platter, or individual serving plates.
5. Melt the butter in a small pan. Remove from the heat and add the paprika, chilli flakes or red pepper flakes and set aside.
6. Heat a good glug of oil in a large frying pan over a high heat. When hot, crack in the eggs and fry until frazzled and crispy.
7. Use a sharp knife to slice open the aubergine, and use a spoon or your hands to scoop out the soft, cooked, smoky centre. Place the pieces of aubergine flesh among the lentils. Dot the lentil mixture with spoonfuls of yoghurt. Spoon over half of the paprika butter, then top each portion with a fried egg and a final drizzle of the butter. Eat immediately.

Artichoke & Roasted Tomato Panzanella

A twist on the more common panzanella (see page 151), made with fresh tomatoes. Choose really good quality artichokes (and definitely not those from a can).

PREP TIME 15 MINUTES • COOK TIME 10 MINUTES
PLUS OPTIONAL 1 HOUR STANDING TIME
SoF / NF / DF / V / Ve • SERVES 4

- 300g (10½oz) day-old ciabatta, torn into bite-sized pieces
- 2 tablespoons extra-virgin olive oil
- 400g (14oz) cherry tomatoes (try to choose different colours, if possible)
- 150g (5½oz) good-quality grilled artichokes in oil (from a jar, not canned), drained well and chopped into 2–3cm (¾–1¼in) pieces
- leaves from 4 bushy sprigs of basil, roughly torn

FOR THE DRESSING:
- 1 tablespoon finely chopped shallot
- 1 clove of garlic, crushed
- a pinch of salt
- 1 tablespoon extra-virgin olive oil
- 1 tablespoon rapeseed oil
- ½ teaspoon sherry vinegar, or to taste

1. Heat the oven to 200°C fan/425°F/gas mark 7.
2. Toss the ciabatta pieces in 1 tablespoon of the olive oil and arrange on a baking tray. Arrange the cherry tomatoes on another baking tray and drizzle with the other tablespoon of oil. Bake in the hot oven for 10 minutes, or until the croutons are golden and crisp and the tomatoes are just beginning to collapse. Remove and set aside.
3. Whisk together the dressing ingredients, then taste – vinegars vary in intensity, so you may need more: it should be tart and zingy.
4. Place the tomatoes, artichokes and basil in a bowl and mix well. If you're serving immediately, add the croutons now and then the dressing, stir well and serve. If you're not serving immediately, wait to add the croutons, as they will become soggy. Either way, add about three-quarters of the dressing to start with, adding more as needed. Leaving the vegetables to sit for an hour will allow the flavours to develop, but it's not essential.

Roast Pumpkin, Labneh & Rocket
with Toasted Seeds & Chilli Oil

Labneh is a homemade cheese made by salting and straining yoghurt until it's really, really thick. Its sourness works brilliantly with sweet roasted pumpkin and warming chilli oil.

PREP TIME 15 MINUTES • COOK TIME 40 MINUTES
PLUS UP TO 24 HOURS DRAINING

SoF / NF / WF / GF / V • SERVES 4

- 1kg (2lb 4oz) pumpkin or squash, peeled, deseeded, cut into chunks or wedges
- 2 tablespoons extra-virgin olive oil
- salt and freshly ground black pepper
- 2 tablespoons pumpkin seeds
- 2 tablespoons sunflower seeds
- 3 big handfuls of rocket
- freshly squeezed lemon juice
- Chilli & Garlic Oil (ready-made or see page 212)
- a pinch of red chilli flakes

FOR THE LABNEH:
- 500g (1lb 2oz) full-fat thick Greek-style yoghurt (or full-fat plant-based plain yoghurt alternative)
- a generous pinch of salt

1. To make the labneh, line a colander or sieve with muslin, set it over a bowl and pour in the yoghurt and the salt. Mix gently to incorporate the salt, then leave for as long as possible to drain and thicken. A couple of hours is fine, but overnight is best – in which case, place the draining yoghurt in the fridge. When it's ready the yoghurt will be very thick.

2. Heat the oven to 200°C fan/425°F/gas mark 7.

3. Place the chunks of pumpkin on a baking tray and drizzle over the oil. Season with salt and pepper, toss, then roast in the oven for 40 minutes, or until tender and beginning to char at the edges. Remove from the oven and allow to cool slightly.

4. Toast the seeds in a dry pan until golden and puffed up.

5. Serve the salad on a platter or as individual servings. Place the rocket on the bottom, then add the roasted squash. Spoon over the labneh, then scatter over the seeds. Squeeze over some lemon juice and pour over a generous drizzle of Chilli and Garlic Oil. Finish with a pinch of dried chilli flakes and a little more salt and pepper.

TIP

Any leftover labneh can be rolled into balls and stored in a jar of olive oil for a week or two, in the fridge.

LEON Kale Caesar

We make a version of this salad and sell it in supermarkets,
so you may have tried it already. It's not a traditional Caesar, but we still love it.

PREP TIME 15 MINUTES • COOK TIME 10 MINUTES

DF / V / Ve • SERVES 4

- 75g (2½oz) pasta (twists or shells)
- salt
- 1½ tablespoons pine nuts
- 1 tablespoon pumpkin seeds
- 1 tablepoon sunflower seeds
- 100g (3½oz) cavolo nero/black kale, ribs removed, shredded
- freshly squeezed lemon juice
- 1 × 400g (14oz) can of cannellini beans, drained and rinsed
- 1 spring onion, very finely chopped
- a handful of fresh flat-leaf parsley leaves, chopped if large
- vegan Parmesan (or regular Parmesan) shavings, to serve

FOR THE DRESSING:
- 2 heaped tablespoons vegan mayonnaise (or use regular)
- 1 teaspoon Dijon mustard
- ½ teaspoon vegetarian/vegan Worcestershire sauce
- 1 teaspoon freshly squeezed lemon juice, or to taste
- 1 teaspoon extra-virgin olive oil
- ½ teaspoon red wine vinegar, or to taste
- 1 small clove of garlic, or to taste, crushed to a paste with the blade of a knife

1. Cook the pasta in boiling salted water until al dente.
2. Meanwhile, toast the pine nuts and seeds in a hot dry pan until golden, just 1–2 minutes.
3. Place the kale in a large mixing bowl and add a pinch of salt and a squeeze of lemon juice, then massage both into the leaves (this will soften them).
4. When the pasta is cooked, drain and add to the mixing bowl along with the cannellini beans, spring onion and parsley.
5. Stir together the dressing ingredients in a separate bowl, then taste – vegan mayos can vary in flavour, so add more salt, lemon, garlic or vinegar, as needed. Add a dash of water if necessary, so that the dressing is easy to pour, then pour it over the salad and toss.
6. Shave over some vegan Parmesan (or regular Parmesan), add the toasted seeds and pine nuts, then toss the salad gently once more. Finish with a little more Parmesan just before serving.

LEON Winter Slaw
with Crispy Chicken

We serve our winter slaw (guess when!) in the winter, as a side. You can definitely have this version on its own, or with anything you like, but we particularly love it with crispy breaded chicken.

PREP TIME 25 MINUTES • COOK TIME 15 MINUTES

SoF / NF • SERVES 4

FOR THE CHICKEN:

- neutral oil, for cooking
- 2–3 tablespoons plain flour (GF/WF if needed), plus extra as needed
- 1–2 eggs, well beaten
- 300g (10½oz) skinless boneless chicken thighs, cut into bite-sized pieces
- 6–7 tablespoons breadcrumbs (GF/WF if needed), plus extra as needed
- Aioli, to serve (ready-made or see page 216)

FOR THE SLAW:

- 80g (3oz) red cabbage, shredded
- 80g (3oz) celeriac, shredded
- 200g (7oz) carrot, shredded
- 50g (1¾oz) kale, shredded
- 200g (7oz) cooked peas
- a big handful of flat-leaf parsley leaves, roughly chopped

FOR THE DRESSING:

- 1 tablespoon horseradish sauce (choose DF as needed)
- 2 tablespoons milk (dairy or plant-based)
- 1½ teaspoons white wine vinegar
- 1½ teaspoons Dijon mustard
- 3 teaspoons freshly squeezed lemon juice
- 3 tablespoons rapeseed oil
- salt and freshly ground black pepper

1. For the chicken, heat a 5mm (¼in) depth of oil in a wide frying pan over a medium heat. Arrange 3 bowls in front of you – one containing the flour, one containing the beaten egg and one containing the breadcrumbs. To minimize waste, don't overfill each bowl – if you need more, just top up as you go. When the pan is hot, turn the heat down slightly. Dip a piece of chicken into the flour first, then into the egg, coating well and allowing any excess to drain away, then roll in the breadcrumbs. Place in the hot pan and cook for 2–3 minutes per side, until golden all over. Don't let the pan get too hot or the crumbs will burn before the chicken is cooked through. Set aside on a plate lined with kitchen paper or a clean tea towel and keep warm while you cook the rest.

2. Place all the slaw ingredients in a mixing bowl.

3. To make the dressing, place all the ingredients in a small bowl, but only add 1 tablespoon of the oil to start with. Whisk together until emulsified (it won't be completely smooth because of the horseradish). Add the remaining oil and whisk in.

4. Pour two-thirds of the dressing over the slaw, toss, and then add the rest, if needed.

5. Serve the slaw as soon as the chicken is cooked, with aioli on the side for dipping.

Roast Parsnip, Roast Grapes, Blue Cheese & Apple

If you love roast parsnips, this could be your dream salad. We love the combination of sweet roasted vegetables and the intensity of roasted grapes with salty blue cheese.

PREP TIME 15 MINUTES • COOK TIME 35 MINUTES

SoF / NF / WF / GF / V • SERVES 4

- 500g (1lb 2oz) parsnips, trimmed, peeled and sliced into 1.5–2cm (¾in) wedges
- 1 tablespoon extra-virgin olive oil
- 1 tablespoon neutral cooking oil
- a pinch of salt
- 125g (4½oz) red or black grapes
- 60g (2¼oz) lamb's lettuce
- ½ tart green apple (such as Granny Smith), cored and finely sliced
- 100g (3½oz) blue cheese, crumbled (or use a plant-based blue cheese alternative – we like the ones sold online at La Fauxmagerie)

FOR THE DRESSING:
- 2 tablespoons extra-virgin olive oil
- 2 teaspoons freshly squeezed lemon juice
- 1 teaspoon sherry vinegar
- a pinch of salt

1. Heat the oven to 200°C fan/425°F/gas mark 7.
2. Place the parsnip wedges on a baking tray and add the oils and a pinch of salt. Use your hands to coat each wedge in oil, then place the tray in the oven and set a timer for 20 minutes. When it goes off, remove the tray, turn each piece and add the grapes to the tray, brushing gently with the oil. Return to the oven for 10–15 minutes, or until the parsnips are tender and golden. Remove from the oven and allow to cool until warm rather than hot.
3. Stir together the dressing ingredients in a bowl.
4. Tumble together the lettuce, apple, grapes, parsnip pieces and dressing, arranging it all on a large platter. Scatter over the blue cheese and eat immediately.

TIP

Make this with any roasted root vegetables you fancy. This is also lovely with the candied walnuts on page 17.

Kale & Cannellini
with Roasted Tomatoes & Tahini

This is earthy and comforting.

PREP TIME 10 MINUTES • COOK TIME 20–22 MINUTES

SoF / NF / WF / GF / DF / V / Ve • SERVES 4

- 500g (1lb 2oz) cherry tomatoes, halved
- 3 tablespoons, plus 1 teaspoon extra-virgin olive oil
- salt
- 150g (5½oz) cavolo nero/black kale, ribs removed, shredded
- 2 × 400g (14oz) cans of cannellini beans, drained

FOR THE DRESSING:
- 2 tablespoons tahini
- 2 tablespoons freshly squeezed lemon juice
- 2 tablespoons Chilli & Garlic Oil (see page 212) or extra-virgin olive oil
- a pinch of salt
- water, to thin

1. Heat the oven to 200°C fan/425°F/gas mark 7.

2. Place the cherry tomatoes on a baking tray and add 3 tablespoons of the oil and a pinch of salt, turning to ensure each piece of tomato is coated. Roast for 20–22 minutes, or until the tomatoes are almost collapsing. Remove the tomatoes from the oven and allow to cool a little.

3. Meanwhile, place the shredded kale in a mixing bowl and add the remaining teaspoon of oil and another pinch of salt. Massage both into the kale gently (this helps to soften the leaves before eating).

4. For the dressing, stir together the tahini, lemon juice and Chilli and Garlic Oil, or olive oil, until smooth. Add a pinch of salt and just enough cold water to thin the dressing until loose and pourable.

5. Add the cannellini beans and the cooled tomatoes to the mixing bowl, then pour over half of the dressing and decant the remainder into a jug for people to add to taste. Toss gently and serve immediately.

White Bean, Roasted Squash, Egg & Crispy Sage

Sage, butter and squash are just a perfect trio. In fact, they're so good that the eggs aren't even essential (and we love eggs, so that says a lot), so if you want a plant-based meal today, just leave them out.

PREP TIME 15 MINUTES • COOK TIME 40 MINUTES

SoF / NF / WF / GF / V • SERVES 4

- 400g (14oz) squash, peeled and cut into rough 3cm chunks
- 4 tablespoons extra-virgin olive oil, plus extra for the eggs
- salt and freshly ground black pepper
- 1 × 400g (14oz) can of cannellini beans, rinsed and drained
- ¼ red onion, finely sliced
- 2 tablespoons freshly squeezed lemon juice
- 2 tablespoons butter
- leaves from 4 bushy sprigs of sage
- 4 eggs

1. Heat the oven to 200°C fan/425°F/gas mark 7.
2. Place the chunks of squash on a baking tray and drizzle over 2 tablespoons of the oil. Season with salt and pepper, toss, and then roast in the oven for 40 minutes, or until tender and beginning to char at the edges. Remove from the oven and allow to cool slightly.
3. Tip the cooled squash into a mixing bowl with the cannellini beans, red onion, a generous pinch of salt and the lemon juice.
4. Heat the remaining 2 tablespoons of oil and the butter in a frying pan set over a medium heat. As soon as the butter is melted, add the sage leaves. Cook for just a couple of minutes, until the leaves are crispy, then tip the whole lot into the bean and squash bowl. Mix briefly so everything is coated in lemony butter and the sage is well distributed.
5. Wipe out the pan, set it back over the heat and add a splash more of the olive oil. Fry the eggs until done to your liking, then serve the squash with an egg on top or alongside each portion (the yolk will almost form a sauce with the butter and sage). Season with black pepper before serving.

Maftoul & Roasted Aubergine
with Chickpeas & Mint

Maftoul is giant couscous – we love a brand from Palestine, called Zaytoun.
You can use any giant couscous if you can't get maftoul, or if you prefer a finer texture,
use regular couscous. Don't add the pistachios until ready to serve – this needs
their crunch, and they'll soften if you add them too early.

PREP TIME 15 MINUTES • COOK TIME 20 MINUTES

SoF / DF / V / Ve • SERVES 4

- 2 aubergines
- 150g (5½oz) maftoul or giant couscous
- 2 tablespoons extra-virgin olive oil, or as needed
- 1 × 400g (14oz) can of chickpeas, rinsed and drained
- a generous pinch of salt
- 2 tablespoons lemon juice, or to taste
- 50g (1¾oz) cucumber, diced
- leaves from 4 sprigs of mint, roughly chopped
- 1 teaspoon za'atar
- ½ teaspoon ground cumin
- 50g (1¾oz) unsalted pistachios, shelled and roughly chopped

1. Set the aubergines directly over a gas flame on the hob or on a hot barbecue (if you don't have a gas cooker, then turn the grill to high and cook them there instead). Cook, turning every 5 minutes or so, until the aubergines are blackened, charred, smoking and collapsing. Remove from the heat, place them in a sandwich bag and seal, to steam and then cool. Set aside.

2. Cook the maftoul or couscous according to the packet instructions, or simmer in boiling water for 6 minutes. Drain, place in a bowl and then add the olive oil and toss so it doesn't stick. Add all the other ingredients, except the pistachios, to the bowl.

3. When the aubergines are cool enough to handle, remove them from the bag and place on a plate. Cut off the stalks and then cut a slit from top to bottom, without going all the way through. Open each aubergine up like a book and then scoop out the creamy white flesh, leaving the charred skin behind. Roughly chop the flesh, then add to the salad bowl. Toss well and then taste – add more salt, oil or lemon juice, as needed.

4. Serve immdiately, with the pistachios tossed through right at the end.

→ *Pictured overleaf*

Halloumi
with Freekeh & Roasted Tomatoes

Freekeh is a toasted green wheat with a slightly smoky flavour, used much like bulgur.
Our favourite, Zaytoun again, is delicious and also supports Palestinian farmers.

PREP TIME 15 MINUTES • COOK TIME 25 MINUTES

SoF / NF / V • SERVES 4

- 400g (14oz) cherry tomatoes, halved
- 4 tablespoons extra-virgin olive oil
- a pinch of salt
- 225g (8oz) cracked freekeh
- 675ml (22fl oz) water
- vegetable oil, for cooking
- 300g (10½oz) halloumi, torn into 2–3cm (¾–1¼in) chunks
- 4 tablespoons finely chopped flat-leaf parsley
- 4 tablespoons finely chopped dill
- 4 tablespoons finely chopped mint
- a generous pinch of ground allspice

1. Heat the oven to 200°C fan/425°F/gas mark 7.
2. Place the tomatoes on a baking tray and spoon over 2 tablespoons of the olive oil. Add a pinch of salt, then toss everything together. Roast in the oven for 30 minutes, or until charred, sweet and collapsing. Remove and set aside.
3. Cook the cracked freekeh in a 1:3 ratio of water. Bring the measured water to the boil in a pan with a lid, then add the freekeh and simmer for 20 minutes until tender. Drain and set aside to cool.
4. Heat a splash of vegetable oil in a frying pan over a medium heat, then add the halloumi chunks and fry for a couple of minutes on each side until golden brown. Remove from the heat and set aside.
5. In a serving bowl, mix together the cooled freekeh, the roasted tomatoes, the herbs, allspice and remaining olive oil. Mix well, then add the halloumi and mix briefly. Taste – you shouldn't need salt, as the halloumi is salty.
6. Serve while the halloumi is still warm.

↪ *Pictured overleaf*

TIP

For a vegan alternative to halloumi, marinate extra-firm tofu in lemon juice and olive oil, then pan-fry and season it with plenty of salt and dried oregano.

4

Whipped Butterbeans
with Roasted Peppers & Walnuts

Perfect for winter, this salad is for when almost everything else is out of season.

PREP TIME 15 MINUTES • COOK TIME 2 MINUTES

SoF / WF / GF / DF / V / Ve • SERVES 4

- 4 tablespoons chopped walnuts
- 2 × 400g (14oz) cans of butterbeans, drained but not rinsed
- 4 tablespoons extra-virgin olive oil, plus extra to serve
- 4 tablespoons water
- a pinch of salt
- 2 cloves of garlic, crushed
- 1½ tablespoons lemon juice
- 3 roasted red peppers from a jar (in oil, not brine), drained and sliced
- leaves from 2 sprigs of thyme
- a pinch of mild red pepper flakes or chilli flakes, to taste

1. Toast the walnuts in a dry pan for 1–2 minutes, until they begin to smell nutty and darken slightly. Remove from the pan and set aside.

2. Place the beans, 2 tablespoons of the olive oil, 2 tablespoons of the water, the salt, garlic and lemon juice into a small food processor or blender, and blitz until completely smooth, adding the remaining olive oil and water gradually until you have the texture you want. It should be easily spoonable – not stiff, but also not runny or wet. Taste and add more salt or lemon juice, if needed.

3. Spoon the whipped butterbeans onto a plate and spread out. Arrange the sliced red peppers on top, then drizzle over a little more olive oil and scatter over the walnuts, thyme leaves and red pepper flakes or chilli flakes.

← *Pictured previous pages*

TIP

Cannellini beans work just as well as butter beans, if you prefer them, or that's all you have in the cupboard.

Chard
with Hazelnuts, Red Pepper Sauce & White Beans

The sauce for this warm salad is what makes it sing – you could swap the greens for spinach, or for something more bitter, such as griddled chicory, or even add in sautéed potatoes.

PREP TIME 15 MINUTES • COOK TIME 10 MINUTES

SoF / WF / GF / DF / V / Ve • SERVES 4

- 200g (7oz) chard, stalks removed, roughly chopped
- extra-virgin olive oil
- 1 teaspoon freshly squeezed lemon juice, or to taste
- 2 × 400g (14oz) cans of cannellini beans, drained
- 4 tablespoons hazelnuts, roughly chopped or crushed
- salt and freshly ground black pepper

FOR THE SAUCE:
- 1 roasted red pepper from a jar (in oil or brine), drained
- 1 small clove of garlic, crushed
- ½ teaspoon sweet smoked paprika
- 2 tablespoons extra-virgin olive oil
- 1 teaspoon sherry vinegar
- a generous pinch of salt
- 3 tablespoons ground almonds

1. First, make the sauce: blitz together the roasted pepper, garlic, paprika, oil and vinegar, along with a generous pinch of salt, until smooth, using a stick blender or a small food processor. Stir in the ground almonds (if you prefer a very smooth sauce, blitz again, but we like the texture the almonds give).

2. Place a saucepan with a lid, large enough to take all the chard, over a medium heat. Add a generous splash of water and the chard, then cover with the lid. Cook for 2–3 minutes, or until the chard has wilted. Drain well.

3. Place the chard in a mixing bowl. Add a splash of olive oil, some salt and pepper, and lemon juice. Toss.

4. Add the drained beans to the empty saucepan and cook, stirring, until warmed through. Keep warm.

5. Set a small frying pan over a medium heat and add the hazelnuts. Cook, stirring often, for just a couple of minutes until they smell toasty – but don't let them burn.

6. Place the chard on a warmed serving dish and top with the beans. Spoon over the red pepper sauce and finally sprinkle over the toasted hazelnut pieces. Eat while warm.

← *Pictured previous pages*

Turkish-Style Bean Salad
with Tahini Dressing

This salad is based on piyaz, a wonderful Turkish bean salad. It's not always made with tahini in the dressing, but we love it for its nutty creaminess (in much of Turkey it would probably not be made with beans from a can, either).

PREP TIME 15 MINUTES • COOK TIME 0 MINUTES

SoF / NF / WF / GF / DF / V / Ve • SERVES 4

- 2 × 400g (14oz) cans of cannellini beans
- 1 small red onion, finely sliced
- 125g (4½oz) cherry tomatoes, quartered
- a big handful of flat-leaf parsley, roughly chopped
- a generous pinch of sumac
- a generous pinch of mild red pepper flakes

FOR THE DRESSING:
- 2 tablespoons tahini
- 3 tablespoons extra-virgin olive oil
- 1 tablespoon lemon juice
- 1 teaspoon cider vinegar
- a generous pinch of salt
- a pinch of ground cumin

1. Drain the beans, reserving 1 tablespoon of the liquid from the can.
2. To make the dressing, place the reserved bean liquid and 2 tablespoons of the beans into a small food processor (or use a stick blender and bowl) along with the remaining dressing ingredients. Purée until completely smooth, then taste. Make the dressing slightly saltier than you think you need it to be and don't worry if the tahini tastes bitter at this point – it mellows out when mixed with the beans.
3. Place the remaining beans (now completely drained) in a bowl with the red onion, cherry tomatoes and flat-leaf parsley. Pour over half of the dressing and toss, then taste, and add more of the dressing if the salad seems at all dry – it should be generously dressed, but not wet and soupy. When happy, top with a pinch of sumac and a pinch of red pepper flakes, then serve.

Spelt, Wild Mushrooms & Green Herbs

Nubbly, nutty spelt grain, with garlicky wild mushrooms and beautifully fresh green herbs.

PREP TIME 15 MINUTES • COOK TIME 35 MINUTES

SoF / NF / V • SERVES 4

- 200g (7oz) spelt grain/pearled spelt
- a knob of butter
- a splash of vegetable oil
- 300g (10½oz) mixed wild mushrooms, sliced
- a big handful of flat-leaf parsley, finely chopped, plus extra to garnish
- 4 tablespoons finely chopped chives
- 2 tablespoons finely chopped fresh tarragon (optional)
- freshly squeezed lemon juice, to taste (optional)
- vegetarian Parmesan, for shaving
- extra-virgin olive oil, for drizzling
- salt and freshly ground black pepper

FOR THE GARLIC BUTTER:
- 60g (2¼oz) butter
- 2 fat cloves of garlic, crushed

1. Mix together the garlic butter ingredients and set aside.
2. Boil the spelt in salted simmering water for 30–35 minutes, or until tender (but definitely not mushy – it has a firm texture even when cooked). Drain and set aside to cool.
3. Meanwhile, set a wide pan over a high heat and add the butter and a splash of oil. Add the mushrooms and brown them all over (work in batches if necessary so the pan doesn't get too crowded). Once the mushrooms are all browned, return them all to the pan and add the garlic butter. Cook for 1–2 minutes, stirring, until the garlic smells sweet rather than raw. Remove from the heat and set aside.
4. Place the spelt in a serving bowl and add the parsley, chives, tarragon and a squeeze of lemon juice, if using. Arrange the garlicky mushrooms on top and shave over some Parmesan. Drizzle over a little extra-virgin olive oil and season with salt and freshly ground black pepper.

Huzarensalade

*We aren't going to apologise for this totally retro salad – heavy on the mayo,
heavy on the carbs, heavy on rich, comforting flavour. This is based on
a Dutch recipe, but we have a secret love for many a mayo-doused salad,
whether cabbage-based, potato-based, or egg-based. In fact, this salad is sometimes
served with wedges of hard-boiled egg, so go for it, if you fancy.*

PREP TIME 15 MINUTES • COOK TIME 12 MINUTES

SoF / NF / WF / GF / DF • SERVES 4

- 200g (7oz) new potatoes, cubed
- 50g (1¾oz) frozen peas, defrosted
- 50g (1¾oz) ham, chopped
- ½ small shallot, finely diced
- ½ crisp green apple, chopped into small pieces
- 1 carrot, finely diced
- 25g (1oz) gherkins, finely diced
- 3 heaped tablespoons mayonnaise (or vegan mayo; check NF/SoF, if needed)
- 1 tablespoon ketchup

1. Place the potatoes in a pan of boiling water and simmer for 12 minutes, or until tender, adding the peas for the last couple of minutes of cooking time. Drain and set aside to cool.

2. Add the cooled potatoes and peas, plus all the other ingredients to a large mixing bowl and stir. Eat immediately, although it will keep in the fridge for a couple of days, if you like.

TIP

Skip the ham and the ketchup
and tear in a fillet of smoked
mackerel as an alternative.

Cobb Salad

The origins of the famous Cobb salad are much disputed. All we can be sure of is that it was first created in Hollywood in the late 1920s or '30s. Traditionally, the ingredients are arranged in rows on the plate, and the egg is hard-boiled and grated. So we can't claim that this tossed version with soft-boiled egg is classic, but nonetheless we really like it a lot.

COOK TIME 18 MINUTES • PREP TIME 20 MINUTES
SoF / NF / WF / GF • SERVES 4

- a splash of olive oil
- 2 skin-on chicken breasts (400–500g/14oz–1lb 2oz)
- salt and freshly ground black pepper
- 3 rashers of back bacon, diced
- 3 eggs
- 2 baby gem lettuces (or 12 leaves of cos or romaine), chopped
- a large handful of watercress
- 100g (3½oz) cherry tomatoes, diced
- 3 tablespoons finely chopped chives
- 150g (5½oz) blue cheese, crumbled
- 2 sustainably sourced avocados (available online or try a 'wonky' veg box), peeled and diced

FOR THE DRESSING:
- 2 tablespoons Dijon mustard
- 2 teaspoons red wine vinegar
- 2 tablespoons extra-virgin olive oil
- 2 tablespoons rapeseed oil
- 2 teaspoons freshly squeezed lemon juice
- 1 clove of garlic, crushed to a paste
- 3 dashes of Worcestershire sauce
- 2 teaspoons caster sugar
- a pinch of salt
- 1 tablespoon water

1. Set a frying pan that has a lid over a medium–high heat and add a splash of olive oil. Season the chicken all over, then place in the pan and cook for 3–4 minutes on each side until well browned all over. Cover, reduce the heat and cook for a further 10 minutes, or until the chicken is cooked through (exactly how long will depend on the thickness of the breasts). For the last couple of minutes, remove the lid, add the bacon and let it crisp up alongside the chicken. Remove both meats from the pan and set aside for the chicken to rest.

2. Meanwhile, simmer the eggs in boiling water for 7½ minutes, then plunge them into cold water. When cool enough to handle, peel and slice each egg into 4 wedges.

3. Make the dressing: start with the mustard and vinegar in a small bowl and gradually whisk in the oils to create a smooth emulsion, then add the lemon juice, garlic, Worcestershire sauce, sugar, salt and water, and whisk again.

4. Place the lettuce, watercress, tomatoes and chives in a mixing bowl. Chop the chicken into bite-sized pieces and add to the bowl along with the bacon. Toss well. Add the blue cheese and avocado and stir once gently – the aim is to keep both in whole pieces rather than becoming mushy.

5. Divide the salad among 4 serving plates and arrange the eggs on top. Spoon over about half of the dressing and serve the remainder on the side.

Radicchio, White Bean, Feta & Roasted Peppers

Radicchio is a wonderful leaf – tinged deep red and pleasingly bitter. You can often find it year-round, but it's particularly useful in autumn and early spring when summer salad vegetables are harder to find. For a dairy-free version, swap the feta for a couple of tablespoonfuls of capers in brine, drained and roughly chopped.

PREP TIME 15 MINUTES • COOK TIME 0 MINUTES
PLUS 30 MINUTES STANDING

SoF / NF / WF / GF / V • SERVES 4

- 125g (4½oz) radicchio, shredded
- 1 × 400g (14oz) cans of cannellini beans, drained and rinsed
- 75g (2½oz) feta cheese, crumbled
- 100g (3½oz) roasted red peppers in oil, drained and roughly chopped
- 4 tablespoons finely chopped dill
- a pinch of salt and freshly ground black pepper
- zest of 1 unwaxed lemon, plus 2 teaspoons freshly squeezed lemon juice, or to taste
- 1 teaspoon red wine vinegar
- 2 tablespoons extra-virgin olive oil

1. Place all the ingredients in a large bowl and toss, gently. Leave to stand for 30 minutes or so, for the flavours to develop and penetrate the beans and to soften the bitter leaves.
2. Taste just before serving to check the salt and lemon levels – add more as needed.

Merguez & Heritage Tomatoes

with Pine Nuts & Pitta Croutons

*Not all supermarkets stock merguez – beautifully spiced lamb, mutton or
beef sausages, originally from the Maghreb – so you might need to make a pilgrimage
to a proper butchers for this one. If you love harissa, skip the cucumber and dill,
and add a big spoonful of harissa paste to the yoghurt sauce instead.*

PREP TIME 15 MINUTES • COOK TIME 15 MINUTES

SoF • SERVES 4

- vegetable oil, for cooking
- 6–9 merguez sausages (depending on their size), kept whole if small or sliced on an angle if large
- a knob of butter, plus extra if needed
- 3 pitta breads, cut into 2–3cm (¾–1¼in) pieces
- 3 tablespoons pine nuts
- 500g (1lb 2oz) ripe, mixed-colour heritage tomatoes or plum tomatoes (at room temperature), chopped into irregular pieces
- salt
- a big handful of flat-leaf parsley leaves, roughly chopped
- 2 teaspoons olive oil

FOR THE YOGHURT SAUCE:
- 200g (7oz) thick plain or Greek-style yoghurt
- 150g (5½oz) cucumber, grated
- 1 clove of garlic, crushed
- 1 tablespoon dill

1. Place a wide frying pan over a medium heat and add a splash of oil. Cook the merguez sausages, turning often, until gently browned and cooked through. Remove from the heat and keep the sausages warm.

2. Wipe out the pan and return it to a low–medium heat. Add a knob of butter to the pan. When foaming, add the pitta and slowly brown for 3 minutes, before turning each piece. Add a little more butter, if needed, and allow the other sides to brown. Just before the pitta is toasted all over, add the pine nuts to the pan and toast them, too. Remove from the pan and set aside.

3. Place the tomatoes on a serving platter and scatter over a generous pinch of salt. Add the parsley and olive oil, and toss once, gently.

4. To make the yoghurt sauce, stir together the yoghurt, cucumber, garlic, dill and another pinch of salt in a separate bowl.

5. Top the tomato salad with the sausages, pine nuts and pitta croutons, then spoon over generous dollops of the yoghurt sauce. Eat while the sausages are warm.

Crispy Duck

with Pears, Bitter Greens & Herby Mustard Vinaigrette

In the UK, pears and bitter greens are both in season over the winter, making this dish just right for colder months, when we still want the crunch of fresh produce. Duck legs can vary widely in size, so judge how many you need while also remembering that the fat will render out so they shrink a little once cooked. If they're enormous, cook three rather than four.

PREP TIME 20 MINUTES • COOK TIME 1½ HOURS

SoF / NF / WF / GF / DF • SERVES 4

- 4 duck legs
- salt
- a big handful of bitter greens, such as rocket, mizuna or mustard greens
- 1 head of radicchio, shredded
- 2 ripe pears, cored and finely sliced (halve the slices if they're very long)

FOR THE HERB VINAIGRETTE:
- 4 teaspoons Dijon mustard
- 4 teaspoons red wine vinegar
- 4 tablespoons extra-virgin olive oil
- 2 teaspoons honey
- 2 tablespoons finely chopped chives
- 2 tablespoons finely chopped flat-leaf parsley
- a pinch of salt

1. Heat the oven to 180°C fan/400°F/gas mark 6.

2. Prick the duck legs all over with a pin – this helps the fat render out and the skin to crisp up. Salt the legs generously, rubbing it all over, then place them on a rack set inside a baking dish. Roast for 1½ hours, basting once after an hour. Remove from the oven and set aside, allowing to cool slightly and rest for a few minutes.

3. Meanwhile, arrange the salad leaves, radicchio and pear slices on 4 individual plates.

4. For the vinaigrette, stir together the mustard and vinegar, then gradually add the oil, whisking to form a smooth emulsion. Stir in the honey, chives, parsley and salt. Add a dash of water if the dressing is very thick.

5. Pull the warm duck meat and crispy skin from the bones and break into bite-sized pieces. Arrange it on top of the salad, then spoon over the dressing. Eat while the duck is still warm.

4

SALADS
FOR
FRIENDS

Crab & Fennel
with Grapefruit & Chilli

Use fresh crab meat for this one and only make it when crab is in season locally to you –
in the UK that means April to November – as out-of-season crab can be ruinously expensive
(as well as less sustainable). Since crab is pricey, we are keeping the portions smallish.

PREP TIME 10 MINUTES • COOK TIME 0 MINUTES

SoF / NF / WF / GF / DF • SERVES 4 WITH OTHER DISHES

- ½ head of fennel, finely sliced, any fronds reserved and roughly chopped
- 1 grapefruit, peeled, flesh finely sliced
- 400g (14oz) white crab meat
- 1 tablespoon finely chopped red chilli
- 2 tablespoons good-quality extra-virgin olive oil
- salt and freshly ground black pepper

1. Arrange the fennel and grapefruit on a platter, then arrange the crab meat on top. Scatter over the red chilli and any reserved fennel fronds. Spoon over the olive oil and finish with a little salt and some black pepper. Eat immediately.

↪ *Pictured overleaf*

TIP

If you can only get a whole crab,
don't throw away the brown meat:
you can use it to make pasta
sauce, with chilli and lemon,
or to add richness to a
seafood curry.

Panzanella

There are so many different recipes for panzanella, an Italian bread and tomato salad. We have chosen one of the simplest here, but you could experiment by adding capers, anchovies or olives, strips of raw or roasted peppers, fresh mint, parsley or cucumber (although try only one or two of these at a time): all are delicious. You can also play around with the bread – some people like to let day-old bread soak in the juices until soft, rather than toasting it in the oven and adding towards the end. It's not really traditional to toss it in oil before toasting it, but we couldn't resist. One thing is crucial, though: this is a summer salad only. Truly, don't bother trying to make it with bland, out-of-season, hot-house tomatoes.

PREP TIME 10 MINUTES PLUS 1 HOUR MARINATING • COOK TIME 10 MINUTES

SoF / NF / DF / V / Ve • SERVES 4

- 400g (14oz) very ripe tomatoes (try to choose different colours, if possible), at room temperature
- salt
- 300g (10½oz) day-old ciabatta
- 2 tablespoons extra-virgin olive oil
- leaves from 4 bushy sprigs of basil, roughly torn

FOR THE DRESSING:
- 1 small clove of garlic, crushed
- 1 tablespoon very finely chopped shallot
- 2 teaspoons red wine vinegar, or to taste
- 3 tablespoon really good quality extra-virgin olive oil (nothing too peppery, or the dressing may be bitter)
- salt and freshly ground black pepper

1. Cut the tomatoes into small chunks, all roughly the same size. Place in a sieve or colander set over a bowl and sprinkle with a generous pinch of salt. Toss gently and leave to drain for up to an hour.

2. Heat the oven to 200°C fan/425°F/gas mark 7.

3. Tear the bread into rough chunks, about 4cm (1½in) in size, and place in a bowl. Drizzle over the oil and toss to coat. Spread the bread in a single layer on a baking tray and cook in the oven for 10 minutes until golden brown and crisp. Remove from the oven and leave to cool.

4. Whisk together the dressing ingredients. Taste – red wine vinegar can be very punchy, or it can be mellow and sweet, so add another teaspoonful if there isn't quite enough.

5. Remove the tomatoes from the sieve and place in a serving bowl. Add the bread (or leave until serving if you want it to be crunchy) and basil, then drizzle over the dressing and toss everything well. You can eat it immediately, but it will taste better if you can let it sit for at least 30 minutes.

⟶ *Pictured overleaf*

1

2

Broccoli, Burrata, Anchovies & Pine Nuts

There is something deliciously thrilling about tearing open a cream-filled burrata and they go brilliantly with salty anchovies. (Although, you can absolutely do this with buffalo mozzarella, if you prefer.)

PREP TIME 5 MINUTES • COOK TIME 6 MINUTES

SoF / WF / GF • SERVES 4 AS A STARTER OR TWO AS A MAIN

- 200g (7oz) long-stemmed broccoli (purple sprouting or Tenderstem), trimmed
- 4 tablespoons pine nuts
- 1–2 burrata, depending on your hunger
- freshly ground black pepper

FOR THE DRESSING:
- 4 anchovies, very finely chopped
- 2 teaspoons freshly squeezed lemon juice
- 3 tablespoons extra-virgin olive oil

1. Steam the broccoli, either in a steamer above boiling water, or in a pan with just a little water in the base, until the broccoli is tender, 2–4 minutes.
2. Set a small pan over a medium heat and add the pine nuts. Toast for a minute or two, then tip out to prevent them from burning.
3. Stir together the dressing ingredients.
4. Strew the broccoli over a serving platter. Place the burrata in the centre, scatter over the toasted pine nuts, then spoon over the dressing. Finish with a couple of twists of black pepper and eat while the broccoli is still warm.

← *Pictured previous pages*

TIP

Vegetarians, skip the anchovies and use finely chopped purple olives, or capers, instead.

Asparagus & Egg
with Caper Dressing

Serve this as part of a bigger spread, or turn it into a little salad-y starter.

PREP TIME 8 MINUTES • COOK TIME 8 MINUTES
SoF / NF / WF / GF / DF / V • SERVES 4

- 3 eggs
- 200g (7oz) asparagus, trimmed and halved lengthways
- a big handful of lamb's lettuce
- lots of freshly ground black pepper

FOR THE CAPER DRESSING:
- 2 tablespoons capers in brine, drained and roughly chopped
- 2 tablespoons finely chopped flat-leaf parsley
- 2 tablespoons finely chopped chives
- 100ml (3½fl oz) extra-virgin olive oil

1. Simmer the eggs in boiling water for 7½ minutes, then plunge them into cold water, to stop them cooking. When cool enough to handle, peel and cut each one into 4 wedges.

2. Steam the asparagus – you can do this over the eggs if you have a steamer basket, or use a lidded pan with a 2–3cm (¾–1¼in) depth of water – until tender, no more than 3–4 minutes. Remove from the heat and set aside.

3. To make the caper dressing, mix the capers, parsley, chives and olive oil together.

4. Arrange the lamb's lettuce, eggs and asparagus on a platter, then spoon over the caper dressing. Finish with a dose of black pepper. (You probably won't need any salt because the capers are salty enough.)

← *Pictured previous pages*

Black Rice
with Edamame, Crispy Tofu & Miso Mayo

This salad has both crunch and punch. Thai black rice is widely available – it's really flavourful and its purple-black colour means it is full of gut-friendly anthocyanins. Don't make the rice in advance unless you can chill it in the fridge quickly after cooking, as it can harbour bugs otherwise. Serve this with a zigzag of Sriracha if you like things spicy.

PREP TIME 20 MINUTES • COOK TIME 30 MINUTES

DF / V / Ve • SERVES 4

- 200g (7oz) Thai black rice
- 200g (7oz) extra-firm tofu, cubed
- 2 tablespoons chickpea (gram) flour
- neutral oil, for cooking
- 200g (7oz) frozen shelled edamame beans
- 6 radishes, very finely sliced
- 200g (7oz) cucumber, cut into thin ribbons
- 2 spring onions, finely chopped
- 2 tablespoons pickled ginger, sliced
- 4 tablespoons roasted unsalted peanuts, roughly chopped
- a generous pinch of black sesame seeds, to serve (or use toasted white sesame seeds)
- 2 tablespoons crispy onions, from a packet

FOR THE DRESSING:
- 4 tablespoons vegan mayo
- 1 teaspoon miso paste
- 1 teaspoon soy sauce
- 2 teaspoons lime juice
- 2 teaspoon sesame oil
- 1–2 teaspoons cold water

1. Simmer the black rice in a small pan of water, covered with a lid, for about 30 minutes (or according to the packet instructions), adding more water if necessary, until tender.

2. Meanwhile, prepare the tofu: place the cubed tofu in a bowl with the chickpea flour and toss to coat. Set a small frying pan over a medium heat and add a splash of oil. When hot, arrange the tofu pieces in a single layer and cook until golden on one side, about 5 minutes, then turn and cook the other side. Remove from the pan to a plate lined with a clean tea towel.

3. Place the edamame in a small pan of water and bring to the boil. Drain and set aside.

4. Whisk together the dressing ingredients, omitting the water, until smooth – make sure the miso is mixed in. Add one teaspoon of water to start with – you want just enough so that it's pourable, but not so much that it's runny.

5. Once the rice is cooked, remove from the heat and tip onto a plate. Spread out to cool slightly.

6. Assemble the salad: arrange the rice in the bottom of 4 wide bowls. Scatter over the edamame, radish, cucumber, spring onion, pickled ginger and chopped peanuts. Place the tofu on top. Drizzle over the dressing, then finish with a pinch of sesame seeds and the crispy onions. Serve immediately.

Harissa Chicken Salad

This is based on a much-loved dish from the LEON menu. In the restaurants, we serve it with aioli rather than the harissa mayo we've used here. You could do the same (see page 216) or you could buy our LEON aioli.

PREP TIME 20 MINUTES • COOK TIME 40 MINUTES

SoF / NF / WF / GF / DF • SERVES 4

- 4 bone-in, skin-on chicken thighs
- 2 teaspoons harissa paste
- 2 tablespoons neutral oil
- 1 red onion, sliced into wedges
- 250g (9oz) celeriac, cut into 2cm (¾in) chunks
- 350g (12oz) butternut squash, cut into 2cm (¾in) chunks
- 150g (5½oz) carrot, cut into 2cm (¾in) chunks
- 1 teaspoon nigella seeds
- 1 teaspoon ground turmeric
- salt and freshly ground black pepper
- 2 big handfuls of baby spinach
- 2 big handfuls of rocket
- 3 tablespoons Pink Pickled Onions (homemade, see page 217, or from a jar, or use sauerkraut)

FOR THE DRESSING:
- 4 tablespoons mayonnaise
- 2 teaspoons harissa paste, or to taste
- 2 teaspoon freshly squeezed lemon juice, or to taste
- Water

1. Heat the oven to 200°C fan/425°F/gas mark 7.
2. Place the chicken thighs on a baking tray and rub them all over with the harissa and 1 tablespoon of the oil. Tip the onion, celeriac, squash and carrot onto a second baking tray, add the nigella seeds, turmeric, 1 tablespoon of oil and lots of salt and pepper, then toss with a spoon until everything is coated (you can use your hands but they will go yellow!). Roast both trays in the oven for 40 minutes, tossing the vegetables and basting the chicken once, halfway through. Remove from the oven and allow to cool until warm rather than hot.
3. To make the dressing, stir the mayo and harissa together in a bowl and squeeze in the lemon juice, then add just enough water – a splash – to thin the dressing until it's pourable. Taste and add more harissa or lemon, if needed.
4. Divide the spinach and rocket among 4 plates or wide shallow bowls, then add some roasted vegetables and a chicken thigh to each. Scatter over the pickled onions (or sauerkraut), spoon over the dressing and add a final pinch of salt. Eat while warm.

Hot-Smoked Trout & Poached Eggs
with Spinach & Watercress

This simple salad feels like spring to us. If you don't want to do croutons, serve it with warm new potatoes, instead. If you want to fancy it up a bit, use the caper dressing on page 155. It's important that you bring the fish up to almost room temperature before you make it – cold fish and warm egg isn't a great combination.

PREP TIME 10 MINUTES • COOK TIME 25 MINUTES

SoF / NF / DF • SERVES 4

- 300g (10½oz) ciabatta or other firm bread, torn into crouton-sized chunks
- 1 tablespoon extra-virgin olive oil, plus extra to dress the salad
- freshly squeezed lemon juice
- 4 eggs (or more, if you're really hungry)
- 3 handfuls of rocket, watercress and spinach
- 200g (7oz) hot-smoked trout, flaked
- leaves from a bushy sprig of dill
- 1 tablespoon finely chopped chives
- salt and freshly ground black pepper

1. Heat the oven to 175°C fan/380°F/gas mark 5.
2. Place the bread and olive oil on a baking tray and use your hands to toss the bread in the oil. Cook in the oven for 15–20 minutes, or until golden and crisp.
3. Place a large, wide pan of freshly boiled water over a medium heat and add a squeeze of lemon juice. When the water is simmering, crack the eggs into the water and poach until done to your liking. Use a slotted spoon to lift them out of the water and place on a plate lined with kitchen paper or a clean tea towel, to help drain off any excess water. Trim away any trailing bits of white to make the eggs look tidy.
4. Arrange the salad on 4 plates. First, place the leaves in a layer and drizzle over a little extra-virgin olive oil and another squeeze of lemon. Scatter over the croutons and the flaked fish, then top with the eggs, dill and chives. Season with a little salt (remembering the fish will be salty) and lots of freshly ground black pepper. Eat immediately.

Chicory & Apple

with Cauliflower & Candied Pecans

This brown-butter dressing is outrageously, life-changingly good. You're going to want to put it on everything. (Just remember to use when freshly made – being butter-based, it will firm up as it cools.) Be aware this won't work with butter substitutes.

PREP TIME 10 MINUTES • COOKING TIME 10 MINUTES

SoF / WF / GF / V • SERVES 4 WITH OTHER DISHES, OR 2 AS A MAIN

- 2 heads of red chicory
- 1 green apple, cored and finely sliced
- 200g (7oz) cauliflower, core and leaves removed, finely sliced

FOR THE PECANS:
- 50g (1¾oz) pecans, whole or roughly chopped
- a knob of butter
- 1 teaspoon maple syrup

FOR THE DRESSING:
- 85g (3oz) butter
- 1½ tablespoons white wine vinegar
- 2 tablespoons Dijon mustard
- salt and freshly ground black pepper

1. First, make the pecans: place a small pan over a medium heat and add the butter and the pecans. Cook, stirring, until the butter is foaming and the pecans begin to smell toasty. Remove from the heat, add the maple syrup and stir to coat. Set aside.

2. Next, make the dressing: melt the butter in a small pan over a medium heat. Once the butter starts to foam, keep an eye on it – under the foam it will slowly begin to turn a golden brown, with a rich nutty smell, but it can also burn quite quickly. As soon as the butter is browned, pour it into a small bowl so that it can't continue to cook. Whisk in the vinegar and mustard, stirring until emulsified. Season with salt and pepper.

3. Separate the chicory leaves, chopping any large ones into pieces, and removing the core. Place in a mixing bowl and add the finely sliced apple and cauliflower (including any small pieces that may have crumbled as you sliced). Pour over the dressing and toss gently, then add the pecans. Serve immediately.

Stacey's Roasted Peaches
with Burrata & Raspberries

This recipe is by Stacey Strachan, one of LEON's people growth managers. She says: 'My friends and I love summer BBQs and I'm always in charge of the salads. A version of this recipe was passed on to me but I've tweaked it so many times for it to become my own. Because we all love buratta so much, I always aim for one ball per person, so you might need to increase it, if your friends are the same!' We've also tried this with vegan goats' cheese (we like Goat-ee by Strictly Roots) and vegan mozzarella (try Bluffala by the same brand) – both equally delicious.

PREP TIME 10 MINUTES • COOK TIME 20–30 MINUTES

SoF / WF / GF / V • SERVES 4–6

- 4 ripe peaches (or use nectarines)
- olive oil, for cooking
- 3–4 generous handfuls of soft lettuce leaves, such as lamb's lettuce or rocket
- leaves from 2–3 sprigs of basil, torn if large
- leaves from 2–3 sprigs of mint, torn if large
- 2–3 fresh burrata (depending on their size), at room temperature
- 3 tablespoons roughly chopped pistachios or whole pumpkin seeds, toasted in a dry frying pan until golden
- 3 tablespoons pomegranate seeds
- flaky sea salt, to serve

FOR THE DRESSING:
- 2 tablespoons balsamic vinegar
- 50g (1¾oz) raspberries, fresh, or defrosted
- 1 teaspoon agave nectar or honey
- 2 tablespoons freshly squeezed lemon juice
- 2 tablespoons extra-virgin olive oil
- salt and freshly ground black pepper

1. Heat the oven to 200°C fan/425°F/gas mark 7.

2. Halve the peaches, remove the stones and place on a baking tray, then brush lightly with olive oil. Roast in the oven for 20–30 minutes until tender and slightly charred and golden on top. (How long they take depends on their ripeness.) Alternatively, cook on a hot ridged griddle pan or on a hot barbecue for about 10 minutes, turning once halfway through, until tender and marked with grill lines. Remove from the heat or the oven and set aside.

3. Place all the dressing ingredients and a pinch of salt and pepper in a glass jar with a well-fitting lid. Fasten the lid and shake hard. Taste – it should be tart and sweet. Make sure the honey or agave has mixed in, and add a little more sweetness, if needed – but don't make it taste like fruit coulis.

4. Serve the salad on a large platter: arrange the salad and herbs leaves over the platter, then the peach halves. Dot the whole burratas on top of the salad, then scatter over the toasted nuts or seeds, and the pomegranate seeds. Drizzle a couple of tablespoonfuls of the dressing over (you can always add more) and a good pinch of flaky sea salt. Eat immediately.

Blackened Fish Taco Salad

Blackening fish is a technique from Cajun cooking – a style associated with Louisiana, although created by Cajun-Acadian peoples who were deported from parts of what is now Canada in the 18th century. It involves coating fish in melted butter and spices, before cooking at a high heat for a short time, so that the spices and butter darken deliciously. Our nod to tacos is that we serve it with crispy tortilla chips mixed in, and a very crunchy slaw with Chilli-lime Mayonnaise.

PREP TIME 20 MINUTES • COOK TIME 5 MINUTES
SoF / NF / WF / GF • SERVES 4

- 4 tablespoons butter, melted
- 4 hake fillets (or other firm, meaty fish)
- Chilli-lime Mayonnaise (see page 79)

FOR THE SALAD:
- 85g (3oz) white or red cabbage, or a mixture, finely shredded
- ¼ red onion, finely sliced
- 1 carrot, sliced into very thin matchsticks (or coarsely grated)
- a big handful of coriander leaves
- 1 sustainably sourced avocado (available online or try a 'wonky' veg box), diced
- juice of ½ lime
- 1 tablespoon extra-virgin olive oil
- salt
- a handful of broken tortilla chips (optional)

FOR THE BLACKENING SPICES:
- ½ teaspoon cayenne pepper
- 1 teaspoon paprika
- 1 teaspoon garlic powder
- 1 teaspoon dried oregano
- ½ teaspoon dried thyme

1. First, prepare the salad. Place all the vegetables and herbs in a large bowl, then squeeze over the lime juice and pour over the oil. Add a pinch of salt and then toss gently. Set aside.
2. Place a frying pan over a high heat, to warm up.
3. Mix together all the blackening spices. Pour the melted butter into a wide bowl and add the fish. Turn the fish, coating it thoroughly in the butter, then rub the spice mixture into the fish, coating it thickly. Once the frying pan is really hot (but not quite smoking), add the fish fillets and cook for about 2 minutes on each side, by which point the outside of the fish should be dark brown and the insides just cooked.
4. Arrange the salad on individual plates, adding the tortilla chips now, if using, and top with the blackened fish. Serve with the Chilli-lime Mayonaise on the side.

Platter Poke

Poke, a sort of deconstructed sushi from Hawaii, is usually served in a single-portion bowl, but we thought it would be fun to serve a big one on a platter – it's a very pretty dish. If you don't eat fish, you could make crispy tofu or replace it with nuts. If you prefer cooked over raw, grilled fish works nicely, as does cooked seafood.

**PREP TIME 15 MINUTES • COOK TIME 12 MINUTES
PLUS 15–30 MINUTES STANDING**

NF / DF • SERVES 4

- 400g (14oz) sushi rice
- 1 tablespoon rice vinegar
- ½ teaspoon sugar
- a pinch of salt
- a pinch of dried wakame seaweed
- 1 sustainably sourced avocado (available online or try a 'wonky' veg box), diced or finely sliced
- 400g (14oz) sushi-grade kingfish, skin and bones removed, cut into 1–2cm (½–¾in) cubes
- 400g (14oz) cooked edamame beans, cooled
- 1 purple carrot, finely cut into matchsticks
- 4 soft lettuce leaves
- a generous handful of coriander leaves
- 3 spring onions, finely diced
- 6 tablespoons ready-made crispy onions
- toasted sesame seeds, to garnish

FOR THE DRESSING:
- 4 tablespoons tamari soy sauce
- 4 teaspoons mirin
- 4 teaspoons sesame oil

FOR THE WASABI MAYONNAISE:
- 3 tablespoons mayonnaise
- 1 teaspoon wasabi, or to taste
- freshly squeezed lime juice, to taste

1. Rinse the rice, then place in a pan with 600ml (20fl oz) water. Bring to the boil, then reduce to a simmer, cover and cook for 12 minutes, or according to the packet instructions. Remove from the heat and allow to steam, covered, for 15–30 minutes.

2. Stir the rice vinegar, sugar and a pinch of salt into the rice, and fluff up with a fork. If not serving immediately, chill it in the fridge until ready to serve, or set aside while you make the rest of the dish.

3. While the rice cooks, rehydrate the dried seaweed in freshly boiled water for 8 minutes or according to the packet instructions, then drain and place in a mixing bowl. Add the avocado and fish.

4. Mix the dressing ingredients together and spoon half of the dressing over the fish. Gently stir to coat.

5. Serve the poke on a large platter, arranging the ingredients in sections. Place the rice on one side of the platter, then the edamame, carrot, lettuce leaves and coriander leaves. Place the dressed fish, avocado and seaweed in the middle of the platter, and then sprinkle over the spring onions, crispy onions and a pinch of sesame seeds. Just before serving, spoon the last of the dressing over the rice and vegetables.

6. Mix together the wasabi mayo ingredients, adding more lime or wasabi, to taste.

7. Place the wasabi mayo in a bowl, to have on the side.

Summer (Roll) Salad

We love Vietnamese-style summer rolls – delicious crunchy vegetables, herbs and glass noodles tucked into a soft, rice-paper wrapper – but they can be fiddly to make. So, we wondered: could we turn them into a salad? Answer: totally. If you don't want prawns, leave them out or switch for crispy fried extra-firm tofu.

PREP TIME 15 MINUTES • COOK TIME 7 MINUTES

SoF / WF / GF / DF • SERVES 4

- 150g (5½oz) thin rice/glass noodles
- 200g (7oz) cooked sustainable cold-water prawns
- 150g (5½oz) soft lettuce, torn into pieces if large
- 2 big handfuls of coriander leaves
- leaves from 3 bushy sprigs of mint
- 200g (7oz) cucumber, sliced into ribbons
- 200g (7oz) carrot, sliced into matchsticks or ribbons
- 100g (3½oz) roasted unsalted peanuts, roughly chopped

FOR THE DRESSING:
- juice of 2 limes
- 1 tablespoon finely chopped red chilli
- 1 tablespoon finely chopped lemongrass
- 1 tablespoon sugar
- 2 cloves of garlic, crushed
- 2 tablespoons water

1. Rehydrate the noodles in a bowl of freshly boiled water for 7–8 minutes. Drain and rinse in cold water, then drain again.
2. Whisk together the dressing ingredients, ensuring the sugar is completely dissolved.
3. Place the noodles in the bottom of 4 wide serving bowls (some noodles plump up more than others, if it looks like too much, don't use them all). Arrange the salad ingredients on top, finishing with the peanuts. Spoon the dressing over the salad and serve immediately.

Emily's Roasted Butternut
with Goats' Cheese, Rocket & Pine Nuts

Emily works in our grocery team. 'I'm from South Africa and this is a salad that my family serves at a braai (a South African barbecue). It goes down a treat. Butternut is a very popular dish in SA, as it's grown locally. The sweetness of the butternut with the saltiness of the cheese works so well with braai meat.'

PREP TIME 15 MINUTES • COOK TIME 40–45 MINUTES

SoF / WF / GF / V • SERVES 4

- 1kg (2lb 4oz) butternut squash, skin on, chopped into 3cm (1¼in) chunks
- 1 tablespoon extra-virgin olive oil, plus extra to dress the salad
- 4 tablespoons pine nuts
- 4 big handfuls of rocket
- 150g (5½oz) rindless goats' cheese
- freshly squeezed lemon juice
- balsamic vinegar, to serve (optional)
- salt and freshly ground black pepper

1. Heat the oven to 200°C fan/425°F/gas mark 7.
2. Tip the squash into a baking tray, add the olive oil and use your hands to rub it all over the squash. Season with salt and pepper and roast in the oven for 40–45 minutes, or until really tender and sweet, and beginning to char on the edges.
3. Remove from the heat and allow to cool to warm or even room temperature.
4. Toast the pine nuts for a couple of minutes in a hot, dry pan – don't let them burn.
5. Arrange the rocket on the bottom of a large platter, then add the squash and the pine nuts. Crumble the goats' cheese over the top, then dress with more olive oil and a squeeze of lemon juice. Season generously with salt and freshly ground black pepper, and a dash of balsamic vinegar if you'd like a bit of extra tang.

Griddled Hispi

with Yoghurt Sauce, Crispy Onions & Brown Butter Almonds

Hispi cabbage is also known as sweetheart or pointed cabbage. When quartered and lightly charred in a pan, it is utterly transformed. Here, we are serving it as a warm salad, with a yoghurt sauce and almonds toasted in brown butter.

PREP TIME 10 MINUTES • COOK TIME 10 MINUTES

SoF / WF / GF / V • SERVES 4

- 1 tablespoon vegetable or rapeseed oil
- 1 large or 2 small heads of hispi cabbage, quartered
- 2 tablespoons crispy onions (from a packet or tub)

FOR THE ALMONDS:
- 2 tablespoons butter
- 4 tablespoons flaked almonds

FOR THE YOGHURT SAUCE:
- 150ml (5fl oz) thick Greek-style yoghurt
- 1 clove of garlic, crushed to a paste with the flat blade of a knife
- 2 tablespoons finely chopped mint
- 2 tablespoons finely chopped flat-leaf parsley
- a pinch of salt
- 1–2 tablespoons freshly squeezed lemon juice, or to taste

1. Place a wide frying pan over a medium heat and add the oil. Place the hispi quarters in the pan, cut-sides down, and cook for 2–3 minutes per side, turning until all the cut edges begin to soften and char. When the hispi is charred on both sides, remove it from the pan and place on a platter.

2. Meanwhile, stir together the yoghurt sauce ingredients. Taste and add more lemon or salt, as needed.

3. Wipe out the pan, return it to the heat and add the butter. When foaming, add the almonds and toast as the butter browns – just for a minute or two, as the almonds will cook very quickly. Remove from the heat and pour the butter and almonds into a small bowl, so that neither burn in the residual heat of the pan.

4. Spoon the yoghurt sauce over the hispi, then scatter over the buttery toasted almonds and the crispy onions. Serve while the hispi is warm.

Mushroom 'Shawarma' Salad
with Pitta Chips

*Of course, this really isn't a shawarma at all – they are always made with meat.
We've just borrowed some of the flavours and some of the spices to make this vegan salad
version deliciously reminiscent.*

PREP TIME 15 MINUTES • COOK TIME 14 MINUTES

SoF / NF / DF / V / Ve • SERVES 4

- 1 tablespoon extra-virgin olive oil, plus extra if needed
- 280g (10oz) portobello mushrooms, thickly sliced
- 1 onion, finely sliced
- 1 teaspoon ground cumin
- ½ teaspoon ground cinnamon
- 1 teaspoon ground turmeric
- 1 teaspoon paprika
- salt and freshly ground black pepper
- 200g (7oz) cherry tomatoes, halved
- 200g (7oz) cucumber, roughly diced
- a bunch of flat-leaf parsley, leaves only, roughly chopped
- Pink Pickled Onions (see page 217), to serve

FOR THE TAHINI SAUCE:
- 4 teaspoons each tahini and lemon juice
- a pinch of salt
- 1 clove of garlic, crushed to a paste

FOR THE CROUTONS:
- 4 pitta breads chopped into 2–3cm (¾–1¼in) pieces (check SoF, if needed)
- 1½ tablespoons extra-virgin olive oil
- a generous pinch of za'atar
- a generous pinch of mild red pepper flakes
- a pinch of salt

1. Pour the olive oil into your biggest frying pan (or work in batches) and set over a medium heat. When hot, add the mushrooms and onion and sauté until beginning to brown, about 8 minutes. Add the cumin, cinnamon, turmeric and paprika and toss the vegetables in the spices. Continue to cook until the mushrooms are collapsing, the onion is soft and it all smells delicious, about another 6 minutes. Remove from the heat, season with salt and pepper, and keep warm.

2. Meanwhile, make the croutons. Heat the oven to 200°C fan/425°F/gas mark 7. Place the chopped pitta, olive oil, za'atar and mild red pepper flakes in a bowl and toss until thoroughly coated. Tip onto a baking tray, spread out into a single layer, and place in the oven for 12 minutes, or until golden and crisp.

3. Stir together all the ingredients for the tahini sauce. If it stiffens up, as tahini often does, slowly thin with a little water until still thick, but pourable.

4. Toss the tomatoes, cucumber, parsley and pitta chips together in a mixing bowl. Divide among 4 plates and top each with the spiced onions and mushrooms, then drizzle over the tahini sauce and drape a few slices of Pink Pickled Onions over each serving. Eat immediately.

→ *Pictured overleaf*

Pinar's Kısır

Pinar Seseogullari works at LEON in Hammersmith, London, but originally comes from Turkey. She was kind enough to give us the recipes for a few of her favourite salads from home. Kısır is a Turkish bulgur wheat and herb salad and is served as part of meze meals throughout the country.

PREP TIME 15 MINUTES • COOK TIME 20 MINUTES

SoF / NF / DF / V / Ve • SERVES 4

- 250g (9oz) fine bulgur wheat
- 200ml (7fl oz) freshly boiled water
- 6 spring onions
- 3–4 cos lettuce leaves
- 30g (1oz) or a small bunch of flat-leaf parsley
- 3 mint leaves
- 1½ tablespoons tomato purée
- 1 tablespoon extra-virgin olive oil
- 1 teaspoon mild red pepper flakes (ideally Turkish pul biber)
- 1 teaspoon ground cumin
- ½ teaspoon salt
- juice of 1 large lemon
- 1 tablespoon pomegranate molasses
- 50g (1¾oz) pomegranate seeds (optional)

1. Place the bulgur in a large bowl, pour over the freshly boiled water and cover with clingfilm or a close-fitting lid. Leave for 20 minutes.

2. Meanwhile, chop the spring onions, lettuce, parsley and mint into small pieces. Set aside.

3. Check the bulgur: if it's cooked it will be tender and the water will have been absorbed. Use a spoon to separate the grains and then add the tomato purée and olive oil. Use your hands to mix, until each grain is coated. Add the chopped vegetables and herbs, red pepper flakes, cumin and salt and mix again. Finally, add the lemon juice and pomegranate molasses, mix once more and serve with the pomegranate seeds, if using, on top.

→ *Pictured overleaf*

TIP

If you have a local Turkish supermarket, this is lovely with a spoonful of hot or mild Turkish red pepper paste, biber salcasi, added with the tomato purée.

4

Roast Carrots

with Dukkah, Cumin-Spiced Hummus & Rocket

At the risk of over chickpea-ing things (is that possible? We think not),
this is fabulous with the roasted chickpeas on page 105 on top. If you like, you can add
a pinch of allspice or a few fennel seeds to your dukkah.

PREP TIME 20 MINUTES • COOK TIME 30 MINUTES

SoF / WF / GF / DF / V • SERVES 4

- 400g (14oz) carrots, washed but not peeled, quartered lengthways (multicoloured carrots look good)
- 1 tablespoon honey
- 1 tablespoon extra-virgin olive oil, plus extra to serve
- a big handful of rocket

FOR THE DUKKAH:
- 25g (1oz) blanched hazelnuts
- 25g (1oz) flaked almonds
- 2 teaspoons sesame seeds
- 2 teaspoons coriander seeds
- 2 teaspoons cumin seeds
- 15 twists of freshly ground black pepper
- ½ teaspoon ground paprika
- a big pinch of salt

FOR THE HUMMUS:
- 2 × 400g (14oz) cans of chickpeas, drained but not rinsed
- 1 teaspoon ground cumin
- ½ teaspoon fine salt
- 4 teaspoons tahini
- 2 tablespoon extra-virgin olive oil
- 4 tablespoons water
- freshly squeezed lemon juice, to taste

1. Heat the oven to 200°C fan/425°F/gas mark 7.
2. Line a baking tray with foil and arrange the carrots on top. Pour over the honey and olive oil, then use your hands to toss until everything is coated. Roast in the oven for 30 minutes, turning once about 10 minutes before the end of cooking. Remove from the oven and cool to room temperature.
3. Meanwhile, toast all the dukkah ingredients, except the paprika and salt, in a dry pan over a medium heat for 1–2 minutes until fragrant but definitely not burnt. Add the paprika and salt and blitz in a small food processor or spice grinder until sandy in texture. Cool, then seal in a tub or jar with a lid (any leftovers will keep for weeks).
4. Place all the hummus ingredients in a small food processor and process until whipped, creamy and smooth. Taste: you may find you want more salt, or even a squeeze of lemon.
5. Use a spatula to remove the hummus from the food processor and spread it over a large serving platter. Arrange the cooled carrots on top, then add the rocket and a couple of generous sprinkles of the dukkah. Drizzle the whole thing with extra-virgin olive oil and some freshly squeezed lemon juice, and serve.

← *Pictured previous pages*

Burnt Aubergine Tangle
with Yoghurt & Pomegranate

This is inspired by the cooked vegetable salads Rebecca learned to cook when she was working in Istanbul and Lisbon. In the UK, we tend to think that salads mean leaves, but that isn't true in other countries. Serve this with flatbreads, or crusty bread, and some raw cucumber, carrot and tomatoes (dressed with salt and olive oil) on the side. Burning the aubergine might sound scary, and can be a bit messy, but it's very easy and the results are more than worth it.

PREP TIME 15 MINUTES • **COOK TIME 15 MINUTES**

SoF / NF / WF / GF / V • **SERVES 4**

- 3 aubergines
- 2 tablespoons extra-virgin olive oil
- 2 tablespoons chopped flat-leaf parsley
- 1 small clove of garlic, crushed
- 2 teaspoons lemon juice
- a generous pinch of salt, plus extra to serve
- 3–4 tablespoons thick Greek-style yoghurt (or plant-based alternative)
- fronds from 2 bushy sprigs of dill
- 2 tablespoons pomegranate seeds

1. Set the aubergines directly over 3 gas flames on the hob (or under the grill, set to its highest heat, or on a barbecue). Cook, turning often, until blistered and charred all over, and beginning to collapse. Remove from the heat and set aside to cool.

2. In a small bowl, mix together the oil, parsley, garlic, lemon juice and a pinch of salt.

3. When the aubergines are cool enough to handle, lay the first one on a plate. Cut off the stem end, then slice gently down the middle, but not all the way through, and open the aubergine up like a book. Carefully pull out the soft smoky flesh, leaving the burnt and blackened skin behind. Place the flesh, which will form long thick strands, into a serving bowl. Repeat with the other aubergines.

4. Dot the aubergine with the yoghurt, gently swirling it into the aubergine (but don't fully mix it in). Spoon over the oil mixture, plus a little more salt, and sprinkle over the dill and the pomegranate seeds to serve.

← *Pictured previous pages*

Halloumi Fries

with Pomegranate, Fennel & Chicory

Is there anything better than the squidgy saltiness of just-fried halloumi? Maybe – when it's coated in a spiced crumb and served with fragrant fennel and bitter chicory. You can make this gluten-free by switching the plain flour for chickpea (gram) flour. We also love this with harissa yoghurt instead of the lemon yoghurt sauce, or with harissa on its own, thinned with a little extra-virgin olive oil. If chicory is too bitter for you, choose any crisp, firm-leafed lettuce.

PREP TIME 15 MINUTES • COOK TIME 10 MINUTES

SoF / NF / V • SERVES 4

- 2 heads of chicory, broken into leaves, core removed, large leaves halved
- ½ head of fennel, finely sliced
- 100g (3½oz) cucumber, thinly sliced on an angle, then halved
- leaves from 3 sprigs of mint, torn if large
- 2 tablespoons extra-virgin olive oil
- 2 tablespoons lemon juice
- a pinch of salt
- 3 tablespoons pomegranate seeds

FOR THE SAUCE:
- 4 tablespoons Greek-style yoghurt
- 1 teaspoon extra-virgin olive oil
- 1 tablespoon freshly squeezed lemon juice
- a pinch of (unwaxed) lemon zest
- 1 small clove of garlic, crushed
- a generous pinch of salt

FOR THE HALLOUMI FRIES:
- vegetable oil, for cooking
- 4 tablespoons plain flour
- 1 teaspoon each ground cumin and paprika
- freshly ground black pepper
- 2 × 225g (8oz) blocks of halloumi, cut into 1cm (½in) fingers

1. Place all the salad ingredients, except the pomegranate seeds, in a large mixing bowl and toss to coat everything in the olive oil, lemon and salt. Set aside.

2. Stir the sauce ingredients together in a bowl.

3. Pour a 1cm (½in) depth of cooking oil into a wide frying pan set over a medium heat. Place the flour and spices in a bowl and gently toss the halloumi fingers in the mixture to coat. Carefully place the halloumi in the hot oil, arranging the fingers in a single layer – you may need to work in batches. After a minute or two, the fries will be golden on the bottom. Use tongs to turn each one and cook the other sides – you may need to turn any thicker pieces more than once to cook the sides, too. Once golden all over, remove from the heat and drain on a plate lined with kitchen paper or a clean tea towel.

4. Divide the salad among 4 plates and arrange the halloumi fries on top. You can either serve the sauce on the side, for dipping, or spoon it over. Scatter the pomegranate seeds over each plate just before serving.

Ras el Hanout Chicken

with Chickpeas & Herbed Bulgur

A weeknight supper of dreams. If tahini doesn't do it for you, the Garlic Yoghurt on page 211, or even some yoghurt mixed with harissa, is very good with this salad.

PREP TIME 30 MINUTES • COOK TIME 50 MINUTES

SoF / NF / DF • SERVES 4

- 8 skin-on chicken thighs
- 3 tablespoons extra-virgin olive oil
- 3 teaspoons ras el hanout spice blend
- a generous pinch of salt and lots of freshly ground black pepper
- 1 × 400g (14oz) can of chickpeas, drained
- 4 banana shallots, quartered lengthways
- ½ teaspoon ground cumin
- a pinch of red chilli flakes

FOR THE BULGUR SALAD:
- 200g (7oz) bulgur wheat, cooked according to packet instructions with vegetable stock in place of water, then cooled
- 300g (10½oz) frozen spinach
- 5 tablespoons finely chopped flat-leaf parsley
- 4 tablespoons finely chopped dill
- 3 tablespoons finely chopped fresh mint
- 2 spring onions, halved lengthways and very finely chopped
- 1½ tablespoons extra-virgin olive oil

FOR THE TAHINI SAUCE:
- 2 tablespoons tahini
- 2 tablespoons lemon juice
- 1 clove of garlic, crushed
- 1 tablespoon extra-virgin olive oil
- water, to thin

1. Heat the oven to 200°C fan/425°F/gas mark 7. Place the chicken, 2 tablespoons of the oil, the ras el hanout and some salt and pepper in a large roasting tin. Rub the oil and seasoning all over the chicken. Roast in the oven for 25 minutes.

2. Tip the chickpeas onto a clean tea towel, fold over, then rub gently back and forth to remove the skins. Discard the skins.

3. After 25 minutes, remove the chicken from the oven and baste. Combine the chickpeas, shallots, the remaining oil, cumin, chilli flakes and some more salt and pepper in a single layer on a baking tray and mix well to coat. Place both trays in the oven to roast for another 20 minutes.

4. Place the spinach in a microwave-safe bowl with a splash of water, partially cover with a lid or plate, and zap for 4 minutes. Set aside and, when cooled, squeeze out the excess water.

5. Stir together the tahini sauce ingredients. It will thicken up, so thin with a little cold water.

6. After 20 minutes, remove the chicken (check the meat is cooked and the juices run clear) and set aside. If the chickpeas are crispy, remove from the oven. Otherwise, roast for a further 5–10 minutes. Fluff up the bulgur with a fork, and mix it with the herbs, spring onion and olive oil.

7. Arrange the salad as follows: herby bulgur on the bottom, then the warm spinach, then the roasted chickpeas and shallots, then the chicken. Finally, spoon over the tahini sauce. Eat while the chicken is warm.

Jacob's Blue Cheese Steak

Thanks to Jacob Kerr, who works at Gildersome LEON, near Leeds, for the inspiration that led to this steak salad.

PREP TIME 20 MINUTES • COOK TIME 8 MINUTES

SoF / WF / GF • SERVES 4

- 225g (8oz) sirloin steak
- salt and freshly ground black pepper
- a dash of vegetable or rapeseed oil
- a small knob of butter
- 50g (1¾oz) chopped walnuts
- 1 teaspoon maple syrup
- 2 sticks of celery, trimmed, sliced lengthways and diced
- 1 head of round lettuce, torn into bite-sized pieces
- 6 radishes, each cut into 6–8 wedges
- 1 small shallot, finely sliced
- 125g (4½oz) blue cheese, at room temperature, crumbled
- 2 tablespoons finely chopped chives
- a big handful of flat-leaf parsley leaves

FOR THE DRESSING:
- 4 teaspoons Dijon mustard
- 4 teaspoons red wine vinegar
- 4 tablespoons rapeseed oil
- a pinch of salt
- water, to thin (optional)

1. First, cook the steak. Season well all over, then place in a very hot pan with a tiny splash of oil – you really want it to sear and caramelize the surface of the meat, rather than spluttering in lots of oil. Cook for about 2 minutes on each side – for this salad, it's best for the meat to be rare, which means it will feel quite soft if you press it with a finger. Remove from the pan and rest on a plate.

2. Melt the butter in a small pan over a medium heat, then add the walnuts and toast for a minute, stirring. Add the maple syrup, toss quickly to coat, then remove from the heat and set aside.

3. Make the dressing: place the mustard and vinegar in a small bowl and gradually add the oil, spoonful by spoonful, whisking with a fork to create a smooth emulsion between each addition. Add the salt and taste to check it feels balanced (remember the nuts will add sweetness to the dish). If it's very thick, stir in a teaspoon or so of water.

4. Place the celery, lettuce, radishes and shallot in a large serving bowl or on a platter.

5. Slice the rested steak thinly, cutting against the grain of the meat, and arrange the warm slices on top of the salad. Crumble over the blue cheese, then add the herbs and the maple-coated walnuts. Spoon over about half of the dressing and serve the remainder on the side. Eat immediately.

Salt Cod & Tomato

This salad is similar to one of the many, many ways that salt cod is eaten in Spain and Portugal. In Portugal, a dish like this would often also contain chopped parsley, chickpeas and wedges of boiled egg. Salt cod is preserved in – you guessed it – salt, and quite a lot of it, so it needs desalinating over a 24–48-hour period. Look for salt cod that is sustainably sourced. If you can't find or don't like salt cod, this also works well with good-quality canned tuna in oil – look for one that is certified as sustainable (albacore and skipjack tend to be the best options, depending on where and how they were caught).

**PREP TIME 10 MINUTES • COOK TIME 0 MINUTES
PLUS 24–48 HOURS DESALINATION
PLUS 20–30 MINUTES STANDING
SoF / NF / WF / GF / DF • SERVES 4**

- 250g (9oz) salt cod, desalinated (see opposite)
- 6 ripe plum tomatoes, about 250g (9oz), deseeded and diced
- 1 red pepper, ribs and seeds removed, diced
- 10 black olives, diced
- ½ small red onion, very finely sliced
- 1½ tablespoons extra-virgin olive oil
- 1 teaspoon sherry vinegar

1. A day or two in advance, desalinate the salt cod. Soak it in cold water in the fridge, changing the water 3–4 times. You can taste the cod to see whether it's ready or not. When it's ready, to be used shred it by hand.

2. Place all the ingredients in a serving bowl, toss and leave for 20–30 minutes for the flavours to meld and develop.

Crispy Pork
with Celeriac Apple Slaw

Roast pork doesn't always need roast vegetables with it – this combination of sweet-sour apple, peppery celeriac and a mustardy sour cream dressing works so well with the richness of pork belly. That said, you could serve this with leftover pork from any cut (warmed up first), or with freshly cooked pork chops. You could also experiment with the slaw: for something sharper, add capers; for more crunch, add diced celery; for sweetness, add the candied pecans on page 162.

PREP TIME 20 MINUTES • COOK TIME 1 HOUR PLUS 15 MINUTES RESTING

SoF / NF / WF / GF • SERVES 4

- 800g (1lb 12oz) pork belly
- salt
- 400g (14oz) celeriac, peeled and sliced into matchsticks
- 1 tart green apple, cored and sliced into matchsticks
- 1 medium shallot, finely chopped (about 4 tablespoons)

FOR THE DRESSING:
- 6 heaped tablespoons sour cream
- 2 teaspoons wholegrain mustard
- 2 teaspoons freshly squeezed lemon juice
- 1 tablespoon cider vinegar
- 3 tablespoons finely chopped dill
- a really generous pinch of salt and 5 turns of the pepper grinder
- 2–3 tablespoons water, if needed

1. Pat the pork belly dry with kitchen paper or a clean tea towel. Use a very sharp knife to score the skin in diagonal lines, then season generously all over with salt.

2. Heat the oven to 240°C fan/500°F/gas mark 10.

3. Place the pork on a rack in a roasting tin lined with foil (this is to make cleaning up easier). Roast in the oven for 30 minutes, then reduce the heat to 180°C fan/400°F/gas mark 6 and roast for another 30 minutes. Remove from the oven and leave to rest for 15 minutes.

4. Meanwhile, prepare the celeriac, apple and shallot and place in a large mixing bowl.

5. Stir together all the dressing ingredients, except the water. When fully combined, thin slightly with water if it seems very thick. Taste and add more seasoning, if needed.

6. Add half of the dressing to the mixing bowl and toss all the ingredients together. You will probably need more of the dressing, but possibly not every last drop, so add it gradually – you want everything to be well coated, but not soupy.

7. Chop the rested but still warm pork into bite-sized pieces. Add to the bowl, toss once and then serve, either on a platter, or individual plates.

Greek Salad

Summer holidays, on a plate. This works best with all the ingredients at room temperature, especially the tomatoes, and is only worth eating when local tomatoes are in season and full of flavour. (We've skipped the usual olives for this version, but you can add them if you like.)

PREP TIME 10 MINUTES • COOK TIME 0 MINUTES
PLUS 15–20 MINUTES STANDING

SoF / NF / WF / GF / V • SERVES 4

- 200g (7oz) ripe tomatoes (cherry work well), diced into 2cm (¾in) pieces, at room temperature
- 1 red pepper, diced into 2cm (¾in) pieces
- 150g (5½oz) cucumber, deseeded and diced into 2cm (¾in) pieces
- 1 small red onion, finely sliced
- 200g (7oz) feta, crumbled
- leaves from a bushy sprig of fresh oregano, or a generous pinch of dried oregano
- a pinch of salt
- 2 teaspoons extra-virgin olive oil
- 1 teaspoon red wine vinegar

1. Place all the ingredients in a serving bowl and gently mix. Ideally, leave for 15–20 minutes for the flavours to marry and develop.

TIP

Vegans rejoice, for we have found a genuinely good vegan feta, called Fetamorphosis, made by a brand called I Am Nut OK. (Buy it online from La Fauxmagerie.)

Pad Thai Salad

We've riffed on Thailand's rightly beloved and delicious national dish, turning it into a noodle salad by adding some extra raw vegetables.

PREP TIME 20 MINUTES • COOK TIME 9 MINUTES
WF / GF / DF • SERVES 4

- 4 teaspoons tamarind paste
- 2 tablespoons brown sugar
- 3 tablespoons fish sauce
- 2 teaspoons sesame oil
- 3 tablespoons boiling water
- 200g (7oz) dried wide rice noodles (Thai folded rice noodles, sen lek, ideally) (check WF/GF, if needed)
- 1 tablespoon vegetable oil
- 1 onion or 2 shallots, finely sliced
- 150g (5½oz) extra-firm tofu, crumbled
- 2 cloves of garlic, finely sliced
- 150g (5½oz) small cold-water prawns, cooked and frozen, or raw
- 2 eggs, beaten
- a pinch of chilli powder
- 150g (5½oz) beansprouts
- 2 spring onions, finely chopped
- 100g (3½oz) Chinese cabbage, finely shredded
- 100g (3½oz) radishes, finely sliced
- 50g (1¾oz) roasted peanuts, crushed
- a big handful of fresh coriander, leaves only
- 4 lime wedges, to serve

1. Stir together the tamarind paste, brown sugar, fish sauce, sesame oil and boiling water, until the sugar has completely dissolved.

2. Cook or rehydrate the noodles according to the package instructions (usually, cover with boiling water for 8 minutes). Drain and set aside.

3. Meanwhile, heat the vegetable oil in a large frying pan or wok over a high heat. When hot, add the onion and tofu, and stir-fry until the onion begins to soften and the tofu begins to brown. Add the garlic, prawns, egg, chilli powder and beansprouts, and stir-fry for another 2 minutes, or until the egg is just about cooked through and the prawns – if they were raw – are pink and piping hot. Remove from the heat and tip everything into a large mixing bowl, to halt the cooking process.

4. Add the spring onions, cabbage, radishes and peanuts to the bowl, followed by the tamarind mixture, and toss really well.

5. Divide the salad among 4 plates or wide bowls and finish each one with some of the coriander leaves. Serve with a lime wedge on the side of each bowl.

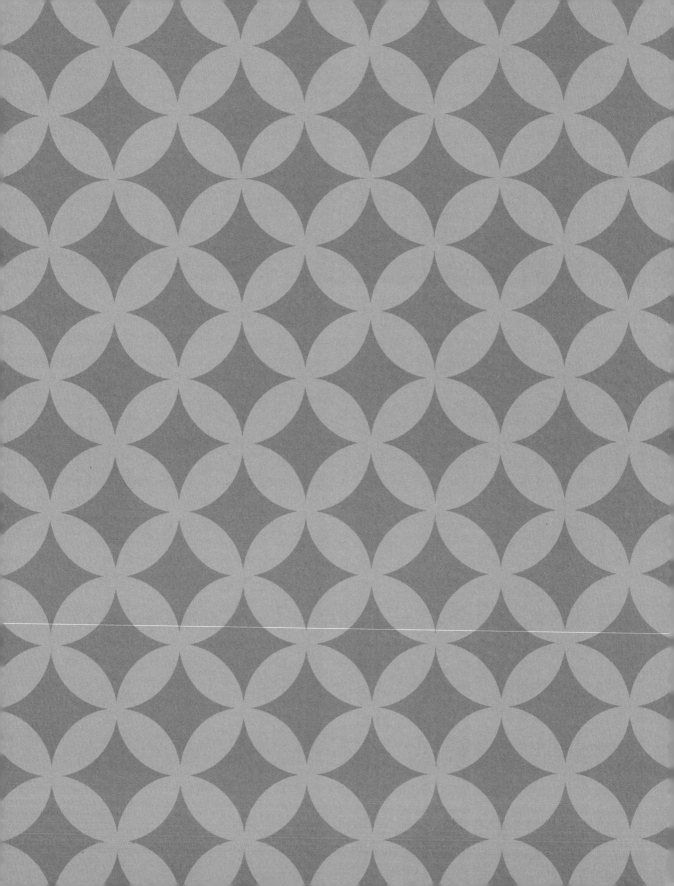

LOVE YOUR LEFTOVERS

Monday-Night Roast Chicken Salad

You are definitely going to want to cook extra potatoes for your Sunday roast, just so that you can make this salad the next day.

PREP TIME 10 MINUTES • COOK TIME 14 MINUTES

SoF / NF / WF / GF • SERVES 4

- a splash of oil, for cooking
- about 700g (1lb 9oz) roast potatoes, cut into 2cm (¾in) pieces
- 600g (1lb 5oz) leftover roast chicken, or as much as you have, skin included, torn into bite-sized pieces
- 70g (2½oz) prosciutto or Parma ham, torn into pieces
- 80g (3oz) watercress, washed and large stalks removed

FOR THE DRESSING:
- 4 tablespoons crème fraîche
- 2 tablespoons finely chopped chives
- 2 tablespoons finely chopped gherkin
- 2 tablespoons finely chopped flat-leaf parsley
- 2 tablespoons extra-virgin olive oil
- 1 tablespoon freshly squeezed lemon juice
- lots of salt and freshly ground black pepper
- up to 2 tablespoons cold water

1. Place a large frying pan over a medium heat and add a splash of cooking oil. Add the chunks of potato and cook, turning after 2–3 minutes, once they begin to crisp up. Move the potatoes to one side of the pan, but allow them to keep cooking, and add the chicken. Sauté, turning often, until it begins to turn golden and the skin begins to crisp up. Push to one side, along with the potatoes, checking that nothing is burning, and add the torn prosciutto. Cook until crisp, just 1–2 minutes. Remove the pan from the heat.

2. Stir together the dressing ingredients, adding just enough water so that the mixture is pourable, but still thick and creamy. (Be generous with the salt, tasting as you go.)

3. Arrange the watercress in 4 wide bowls. Scatter the crispy potatoes on top, then top with the chicken and prosciutto. Dot small spoonfuls of the dressing over each portion and serve immediately.

TIP

If you don't have watercress, use cos lettuce or rocket. If you don't have chicken, this is also good with freshly cooked, firm-fleshed fish, such as mullet fillets, or even trout.

Mackerel & Sautéed Potatoes

with Dill, Radishes & Pink Pickled Onions

This is a great recipe for using up leftover potatoes (although it works almost as well with plain boiled potatoes), which makes it very quick to prepare. There's something magical about smoked mackerel in combination with crisp vegetables, like radishes, and sour flavours, like Pink Pickled Onions (see page 217). Try to bring everything up to room temperature before assembling, otherwise the cold fish and vegetables will contrast too strongly with the warm potatoes.

COOK TIME 20 MINUTES • PREP TIME 15 MINUTES

SoF / NF / WF / GF • SERVES 4

- 500g (1lb 2oz) leftover cooked or uncooked new potatoes (or charlotte or baby potatoes), halved or quartered if large
- salt, for the cooking water
- a splash of oil, for cooking
- 2 generous handfuls of watercress
- 150g (5½oz) radishes, finely sliced
- 150g (5½oz) cucumber, cut into wafer-thin slices
- 1 teaspoon freshly squeezed lemon juice
- 3 tablespoons extra-virgin olive oil
- 3 tablespoons sour cream (or plant-based alternative)
- 4 smoked mackerel fillets
- leaves from 6 bushy sprigs of dill
- 80g (3oz) Pink Pickled Onions (from a jar, or see page 217)
- salt and freshly ground black pepper

1. If using uncooked potatoes cook them in a pan of boiling salted water until tender, about 12 minutes. Drain.

2. Place a frying pan over a medium heat and add a splash of cooking oil. Sauté the potatoes, turning often, until golden all over. Remove with a slotted spoon, draining the oil back into the pan, and set aside. Allow to cool a little – they should be warm, but not hot, when added to the salad.

3. Meanwhile, make the rest of the salad. Place the watercress, radishes and cucumber in a bowl. Mix together the lemon juice and 2 tablespoons of the extra-virgin olive oil and add a little salt and pepper. Taste, then spoon half of the mixture over the salad vegetables and toss.

4. Stir together the sour cream and remaining tablespoon of extra-virgin olive oil, add a pinch of salt and lots of freshly ground black pepper. If it needs thinning, add a teaspoon of cold water, or just enough to make it drizzable.

5. Divide the dressed vegetables between 4 plates. Flake the mackerel into chunks and arrange on top of the salad. Scatter over the dill fronds and the warm potatoes, then the Pink Pickled Onions. Drizzle the sour cream dressing over sparingly, then serve.

Wild Mushrooms & Cheese

with Rocket, Watercress & Sourdough Crumbs

A salad for a wintery day – and the best use for stale bread.

PREP TIME 10 MINUTES • COOK TIME 20 MINUTES

SoF / NF / V • SERVES 4

- 4 tablespoons extra-virgin olive oil, plus extra to serve
- 400g (14oz) mixed wild mushrooms, roughly chopped
- 2 cloves of garlic, crushed
- a generous knob of butter
- 200g (7oz) day-old or stale sourdough, chopped or torn into small croutons
- 4 handfuls of rocket
- 2 handfuls of watercress
- 100g (3½oz) mature crumbly cheese (something like a good-quality, well-matured Lancashire, Cheddar or Cheshire will work well)
- 3 tablespoons finely chopped chives
- freshly squeezed lemon juice
- salt and freshly ground black pepper

1. Pour 2 tablespoons of the oil into a wide frying pan set over a medium heat. Add the mushrooms and cook, stirring often, until golden brown (if your pan is small and the mushrooms are crowded, they'll stew rather than brown, so work in batches, keeping the cooked mushrooms warm in a low oven). When the mushrooms are almost done, add the garlic and the butter, plus some salt and pepper, and cook for a minute or so, until the butter is melted and coating the mushrooms, and the garlic smells sweet rather than raw. Set aside and keep warm.

2. Pour the remaining 2 tablespoons of oil into a wide pan (ideally, use the one you cooked the mushrooms in), then add the sourdough pieces. Cook over a low heat, stirring often, until deeply golden.

3. Divide the rocket and watercress among 4 serving plates or wide bowls. Add the garlic mushrooms, then scatter over the croutons and crumble the cheese on top. Sprinkle over the chives, then squeeze over a little lemon juice and a splash of olive oil to serve.

Roast Lamb

with Crispy New Potatoes, Lamb's Lettuce & Salsa Verde

We love using up leftovers by smothering them in salsa verde. We are also rather pleased with this potato roasting technique – by crushing them and tossing with oil before cooking, you get more of the best bits: crispy edges. Warming the lamb in a foil pouch means it's less likely to dry out.

PREP TIME 15 MINUTES • COOKING TIME 42 MINUTES

SoF / NF / WF / GF / DF • SERVES 4

- 700g (1lb 9oz) new potatoes, halved
- 6 tablespoons extra-virgin olive oil (choose one that is mild, rather than bitter or peppery)
- 6 tablespoons neutral oil
- about 500g (1lb 2oz) leftover roast lamb (or less, if that's what you have), roughly shredded, plus any leftover jus or pan juices from cooking it
- a large handful of flat-leaf parsley leaves, finely chopped
- leaves from a bushy sprig of fresh mint, finely chopped
- leaves from a bushy sprig of fresh basil, finely chopped
- 1 teaspoon Dijon mustard
- 2 teaspoons sherry vinegar
- 2 tablespoons capers in brine, drained and finely chopped
- 1 small clove of garlic, crushed to a paste with the flat of a knife
- 1 tablespoon finely chopped shallot
- 120g (4½oz) lamb's lettuce
- salt

1. Heat the oven to 200°C fan/425°F/gas mark 7.
2. Cook the new potatoes in a pan of boiling salted water for about 12 minutes, or until tender.
3. Drain the potatoes and roughly crush with a potato masher. Add 4 tablespoons of the olive oil and 2 tablespoons of the neutral oil, plus a generous pinch of salt. Toss the potatoes until the oil is well distributed. Tip onto a baking tray and cook in the hot oven for 20–30 minutes, or until golden and the edges are beginning to crisp up.
4. Warm the lamb: make a parcel out of foil that will enclose the lamb completely. Before closing it, add a few spoonfuls of any cooking liquor or jus that you have left over, or a couple of tablespoonfuls of water. Seal firmly and place in the hot oven for 15 minutes. (The lamb should be at 73°C/163°F if you have a meat thermometer; if not, just ensure it is piping hot.)
5. Stir together the herbs, mustard, vinegar, capers, garlic and shallot with 2 tablespoons of the olive oil and 4 tablespoons of the neutral oil. Taste – it should be sharp and piquant.
6. Remove the lamb and potatoes from the oven. Cool slightly, just so that their heat won't wilt the lamb's lettuce. Toss the potatoes and the lettuce together, then divide among serving plates. Top with the warm lamb and a couple of spoonfuls of the salsa verde.

Pork & Gochujang Salad

If you haven't cooked with gochujang before, you're in for a treat. Gochujang is a fermented Korean chilli paste with an umami-filled, sweet-and-spicy flavour, made with soy beans, rice and salt. A tub will keep for months in the fridge and since it makes fantastic broths, noodles, eggs and even sandwiches, it's a worthwhile investment.

PREP TIME 17 MINUTES • COOK TIME 4 MINUTES

NF / WF / GF / DF • SERVES 4

- 125g (4½oz) green beans, chopped into 3cm (1in) pieces
- 400g (14oz) leftover roast or cooked pork (pork belly works brilliantly), shredded or diced
- 100g (3½oz) cos, baby gem or romaine lettuce, shredded
- 100g (3½oz) radishes, finely sliced
- 1 carrot, peeled and cut into julienne matchsticks
- ½ red onion, finely sliced
- 125g (4½oz) cucumber, cut into matchsticks
- a handful of fresh coriander leaves

FOR THE DRESSING:
- 2 teaspoons lime juice
- 4 teaspoons vegetable oil
- 4 teaspoons gochujang (Korean chilli paste) (check WF/GF/NF, if needed)
- 2 cloves of garlic, crushed to a paste with the flat blade of a knife
- 2 tablespoons sesame oil
- 2 teaspoons maple syrup
- 2 teaspoons fish sauce
- 2 teaspoons tamari soy sauce (check WF/GF, if needed)
- 1–2 tablespoons water

1. Stir together the dressing ingredients, except the water, then thin as needed – you want it to be just pourable.

2. Add the green beans to a pan of boiling water over a medium heat and blanch for 1 minute until slightly softened. Drain, plunge into icy water to cool and leave to dry.

3. Place the leftover pork in a wide frying pan set over a medium heat. If it's a fatty cut, like belly, you probably won't need any oil. Sauté for 3–4 minutes, or until piping hot, being careful not to dry out the meat. If necessary, add a tablespoon of water to the pan and cover with a lid.

4. Place all the salad ingredients, apart from the pork and coriander leaves, in a large bowl and toss. Then add the pork and toss again. Divide among serving plates and spoon over some of the dressing. Top with a few coriander leaves. Eat while the pork is still warm.

BLT Salad

with Crispy Potatoes

A BLT – but better. And this one uses up leftover potatoes, too.

PREP TIME 15 MINUTES • COOK TIME 20 MINUTES

SoF / NF / WF / GF • SERVES 4

- 300g (10½oz) back bacon, diced into 1–2cm (½–¾in) pieces
- 400g (14oz) leftover cooked baby new potatoes, halved or quartered into small bite-sized pieces (or cook potatoes from scratch, as described)
- 12 romaine lettuce leaves, chopped
- 175g (6oz) cherry tomatoes, quartered
- 3 tablespoons finely chopped chives

FOR THE DRESSING:
- 4 heaped tablespoons mayonnaise
- 4 heaped tablespoons sour cream
- 1 teaspoon garlic granules (or use 1 small garlic clove, blanched in boiling water for 3 minutes, then crushed to a paste with the flat blade of a knife)
- 1 tablespoon freshly squeezed lemon juice
- a pinch of salt
- 1–3 teaspoons water

1. Pan-fry the bacon in a dry pan set over a medium heat, until the bacon is golden and the fat has rendered out. Be careful not to brown it so much that the meat becomes bitter – it will become crispier as it cools. Remove from the pan with a slotted spoon, leaving the fat behind in the pan (don't throw it away). Set the bacon aside.

2. If using uncooked potatoes, boil in simmering salted water for 12 minutes, or until tender, then drain and allow to steam dry for a few minutes. Place the pan, still containing the bacon fat, back over a medium heat and add the cooked potatoes. Sauté, turning them often, for about 5 minutes, until golden in places. Remove from the heat and set aside.

3. Place the lettuce, cherry tomatoes and half of the chives in a serving bowl.

4. To make the dressing, stir together the mayo, sour cream, garlic granules, lemon juice and a pinch of salt. Add just enough cold water to thin the dressing, keeping it thick, but just about pourable. Taste to check the seasoning.

5. Add the bacon and potatoes to the salad bowl. Toss, then spoon over some of the dressing. Decide whether you want to toss to coat everything, or not. Finish with the remaining chopped chives. Eat while the potatoes are still warm.

6

All recipes serve 4 unless otherwise stated

•

All recipes prepped in 10 minutes or less

Dressings & Crunchy Things

French Vinaigrette

SoF / NF / WF / GF / DF / V / Ve

- 4 teaspoons Dijon mustard
- 4 teaspoons red wine vinegar
- 4 tablespoons rapeseed oil or very mild olive oil
- a pinch of salt
- cold water

Stir together the mustard and vinegar, then very slowly add the oil, whisking to form a smooth emulsion. Finish with a pinch of salt and thin with a little cold water, to make the dressing a pouring consistency.

Balsamic Vinaigrette

SoF / NF / WF / GF / DF / V / Ve

- 4 tablespoons extra-virgin olive oil
- 1 tablespoon balsamic vinegar
- a pinch of salt

Shake the ingredients together in a jar with a lid. The mixture will separate, but that's okay. (If you want to get fancier, you can of course experiment with adding Dijon mustard or honey, but this is the simple, traditional recipe.)

Blue Cheese Dressing

SoF / NF / WF / GF / V

- 75g (2½oz) blue cheese
- ½ teaspoon garlic powder
- 1 tablespoon lemon juice
- 3 tablespoons good-quality mayonnaise
- 5 tablespoons sour cream
- 1 tablespoon extra-virgin olive oil
- 2 tablespoons finely chopped chives
- 2–3 tablespoons milk or (even better) buttermilk
- salt and freshly ground black pepper

Depending on how smooth you like your dressing, you can make this by stirring/beating in a bowl, or blitzing with a stick blender. Combine everything, except the milk and seasoning, and blitz. Add enough milk to loosen, but don't make it wet. Season to taste. Leftovers will keep in the fridge for a couple of days.

Garlic Yoghurt

SoF / NF / WF / GF / V

- 6 heaped tablespoons thick plain or Greek-style yoghurt
- a pinch of salt
- 1 clove of garlic, crushed to a paste with the flat blade of a knife (blanch for 3 minutes in boiling water for a more mellow flavour)

Stir the ingredients together until smooth.

Honey & Mustard Dressing

SoF / NF / WF / GF / DF / V

- 2 tablespoons Dijon mustard
- 2 teaspoon white wine vinegar
- 4 tablespoons rapeseed oil
- 2 teaspoons honey
- a pinch of salt
- water

Stir together the mustard and vinegar, then very slowly add the oil, whisking to form a smooth emulsion. Stir in the honey, mixing thoroughly. Finish with a pinch of salt and thin with a little cold water, if needed, to make the dressing a pouring consistency.

Chilli & Garlic Oil

makes 1 × 1-litre (1¾ pint) bottle

SoF / NF / WF / GF / DF / V / Ve

- 1 litre (1¾ pints) extra-virgin olive oil
- 10 whole black peppercorns
- zest of 1 lemon, shaved using a peeler
- 5 bay leaves, ideally fresh
- 6 red chillies, a mixture of sizes (smaller chillies tend to be hotter)
- 1 teaspoon dried red chilli flakes
- 4 cloves of garlic, sliced
- generous pinch of flaky sea salt

Sterilize a heatproof glass jar or wide-mouthed bottle with a lid (see Pink Pickled Onions on page 217 for method). Place a little of the oil into a large pan and set over a medium heat. Add the peppercorns, lemon zest and bay leaves, then lightly bruise the chillies and cut a slit into one side of each one but leave whole. Add the chillies to the pan along with the chilli flakes and garlic slices. Cook for 2 minutes, then add the rest of the oil and salt. Mix and then allow the oil to warm until hot but nowhere near boiling. Remove from the heat. While still hot, carefully pour into the prepared jar or bottle and seal. Leave for a couple of weeks, somewhere cool and away from bright light, shaking every few days. The longer you leave it, the better the flavours will develop. It will keep for several months.

Herb Vinaigrette

SoF / NF / WF / GF / DF / V / Ve

- 1 tablespoon Dijon mustard
- 2 teaspoons red wine vinegar
- 4 tablespoons extra-virgin olive oil
- 2 tablespoons very finely chopped chives
- 2 tablespoons very finely chopped flat-leaf parsley (or mixture of any soft green herbs – try chervil, tarragon or fennel greens)
- cold water

Stir together the mustard and red wine vinegar, then slowly add the olive oil, whisking to form a smooth emulsion. Stir in the chopped herbs and add a dash of water, if needed, to thin the dressing slightly.

Peanut & Chilli Dressing

SoF / WF / GF / DF

- 3 tablespoons peanuts, roughly crushed
- 3 lime leaves, very finely chopped
- 1 tablespoon finely chopped hot red chilli
- 1 clove of garlic, crushed
- 1 tablespoon sugar
- 2 tablespoons fish sauce
- 1 tablespoon water

Stir all the ingredients together.

Green Goat Dressing

NF / WF / GF / V

- 3–4 tablespoons soft and creamy rindless goats' cheese
- 1 tablespoon roughly chopped chives
- 1 tablespoon roughly chopped dill
- 1 tablespoon roughly chopped flat-leaf parsley
- a small handful of watercress, roughly chopped
- 1 teaspoon cider vinegar
- 1 teaspoon white miso (check WF/GF, if needed)
- 1 tablespoon full-fat plain yoghurt
- 1 small clove of garlic (optional)
- a pinch of salt, if needed

Place all the dressing ingredients into a small jug blender, or use a stick blender. Whizz until bright green and really smooth. Taste and add more salt, as needed.

Caesar-ish Dressing

SoF / NF / WF / GF

- 3 tablespoons sour cream or crème fraîche
- 2 teaspoons finely chopped flat-leaf parsley
- 1 teaspoon extra-virgin olive oil
- a pinch of zest from an unwaxed lemon, plus ½ teaspoon juice
- ½ teaspoon Dijon mustard
- 1 teaspoon finely chopped chives
- 2 anchovies in oil, very finely chopped and then smooshed to a paste
- 1 tablespoon good-quality mayonnaise
- water, as needed

Mix all the dressing ingredients together until smooth, then taste and add more seasoning or lemon, as needed. Thin with water, if necessary.

Vegan Caesar-ish Dressing

SoF / NF / WF / GF / DF / V / Ve

- 4 heaped tablespoons vegan mayonnaise (check Sof/NF, if needed)
- 2 teaspoon Dijon mustard
- ½ teaspoon vegan Worcestershire sauce (check SoF, if needed)
- 2 teaspoons freshly squeezed lemon juice
- 2 teaspoons extra-virgin olive oil
- 1 teaspoon red wine vinegar
- 1 clove of garlic, crushed to a paste with the blade of a knife

Mix all the ingredients together. Taste and adjust the seasoning, as needed.

Orange & Honey Dressing

SoF / NF / WF / GF / DF / V

- juice of ½ orange
- ½ teaspoon honey
- 1 teaspoon cider vinegar
- a pinch of salt
- 2 tablespoons extra-virgin olive oil

Mix all the ingredients together. Taste and adjust the seasoning, as needed.

Fish Sauce, Chilli, Lime & Honey Dressing

NF / WF / GF / DF

- 2 tablespoons fish sauce, or to taste
- zest of ¼ lime, plus 3 tablespoons freshly squeezed juice, or to taste
- 1 tablespoon cold water
- 1 teaspoon rapeseed oil
- 1 teaspoon toasted sesame oil
- ½ teaspoon tamari (check WF/GF, if needed), or to taste
- ½ teaspoon honey
- 1cm (½in) piece of fresh ginger, peeled and finely grated
- 1 clove of garlic, crushed
- ½–1 red chilli (hot or mild, to taste), deseeded and ribs removed, finely chopped

Mix all the ingredients together. Taste and adjust the lime juice, tamari or fish sauce levels, as needed.

Tahini Dressing

SoF / NF / WF / GF / DF / V / Ve

- 2 tablespoons tahini
- 2 tablespoons lemon juice
- 1 clove of garlic, crushed
- 1 tablespoon extra-virgin olive oil
- water
- salt, to taste

Stir the tahini, lemon, garlic and oil together. The mixture may thicken up. Gradually add just enough cold water to thin it to pouring consistency and season with salt to taste.

Chipotle Dressing

SoF / NF / WF / GF / DF / V / Ve

- 1 teaspoon chipotle paste
- 3 tablespoons extra-virgin olive oil
- 2 tablespoons vegetable or rapeseed oil
- juice of 1 lime
- 1 shallot, very finely diced
- 2 teaspoons honey
- 1 teaspoon sherry vinegar
- ¼ teaspoon ground cumin
- a generous pinch of salt and lots of freshly ground black pepper

Whisk together all the dressing ingredients. Taste – it should be sharp, sweet, spicy and just a little bit salty, all at once.

Anchovy & Caper Dressing

SoE / NF / WF / GF / DF

- 2–3 tablespoons extra-virgin olive oil (nothing peppery)
- 3 anchovies in oil, very well drained, finely chopped, then crushed to paste with the flat blade of a knife
- 1 spring onion, halved lengthways and very finely chopped, or 2 tablespoons finely chopped chives, for a milder flavour
- 1 tablespoon capers in brine, drained and finely chopped
- 1 small clove of garlic, crushed
- 1 teaspoon sherry vinegar

Stir together the dressing ingredients and taste. If it looks very thick, add a little more olive oil. If it needs more zing, add a touch more vinegar – it should be salty and tart.

Harissa Mayo

SoF / NF / WF / GF / DF / V

- 2 teaspoons harissa paste
- freshly squeezed lemon juice
- 4 tablespoons mayonnaise (can be Ve)

Beat the harissa paste and lemon juice into the mayo until completely combined.

Vegan Mayo

makes about 250ml (9fl oz)

SoF / NF / WF / GF / DF / V / Ve

- 2 teaspoons cider vinegar
- 1 teaspoon lemon juice
- ¾ teaspoon mustard powder
- ¼ teaspoon salt
- 3 tablespoons reduced aquafaba (aquafaba is the liquid from a can of chickpeas, reduced by half in a small saucepan over a medium heat)
- 5 chickpeas
- 150ml (5fl oz) rapeseed, sunflower or vegetable oil

Place the vinegar, lemon juice, mustard powder, salt, aquafaba and chickpeas into a tall narrow container into which a stick blender will fit, and blitz until smooth, pale and completely combined. Slowly, slowly trickle the oil into the container, with the blender running. It may take up to 5 minutes, but the mixture should start to thicken and turn white as you gradually add the oil. This will keep, covered or in a jar with a lid, in the fridge for up to 5 days.

Vegan Aioli

SoF / NF / WF / GF / DF / V / Ve

- 4 heaped tablespoons vegan mayonnaise
- 1 clove of garlic, crushed to a paste
- ½ teaspoon Dijon mustard
- 1 teaspoon extra-virgin olive oil

Place the mayonnaise in a bowl. Add the garlic, Dijon mustard and extra-virgin olive oil and whisk thoroughly to combine. Taste – add more mustard or olive oil for a stronger flavour.

Tahini Yoghurt Dressing

SoF / NF / WF / GF / V

- 2 tablespoons tahini
- 3 tablespoons plain yoghurt (can be DF, but check if SoF/NF, as needed)
- a pinch of salt
- 1 teaspoon lemon juice, or more to taste
- water

Whisk together the tahini and yoghurt until smooth. Add a pinch of salt and the lemon juice, then slowly add enough water to make the dressing thick but pourable. This will keep for 3 or 4 days, covered, in the fridge.

Ranch Dressing

SoF / NF / WF / GF / V

- 4 heaped tablespoons good-quality mayonnaise (can be Ve) or for a very tangy dressing use 5 tablespoons plain yoghurt (can be DF)
- 2 teaspoons very finely chopped dill
- 1½ tablespoons very finely chopped flat-leaf parsley
- 1½ tablespoons very finely chopped chives
- ¼ teaspoon garlic powder
- 1 teaspoon cider vinegar, or to taste
- 1 teaspoon lemon juice, or to taste
- 2 tablespoons milk (can be DF), or more as needed

Place the mayo (or yoghurt) in a bowl. Add the dill, parsley, chives, garlic powder, cider vinegar and lemon juice, and stir together. Add the milk and mix. Slowly add more milk as needed, until the dressing is as thick as honey. Taste and add more vinegar, lemon, salt or pepper, as necessary. Use immediately, or it will keep, covered, in the fridge for a couple of days.

Smoky Spanish Dressing

SoF / NF / WF / GF / DF / V / Ve

- 1 clove of garlic, crushed
- 2 teaspoons smoked paprika
- 2 tablespoons sherry vinegar
- zest and juice of 2½ oranges
- 1 tablespoon chopped thyme
- 100ml (3½fl oz) olive oil
- ¼ teaspoon black pepper
- ¼ teaspoon salt

Shake everything together in a jar. Taste and add more salt, if needed.

Whipped Feta

SoF / NF / WF / GF / V

- 100g (3½oz) feta cheese, crumbled
- 100g (3½oz) Greek-style yoghurt

Place the ingredients into a food processor or blender and process until completely smooth. Use immediately or keep in the fridge for a couple of days.

Aioli

SoF / NF / WF / GF / DF / V

- 1 fresh free-range organic egg yolk, at room temperature
- ½ clove of garlic (blanched in boiling water for 3 minutes for a more mellow flavour), crushed to a paste with the flat blade of a knife
- a tiny pinch of English mustard powder
- a tiny pinch of salt
- 4 tablespoons olive oil (choose one with a light flavour)
- 4 tablespoons neutral oil
- freshly squeezed lemon juice

Place the egg yolk in a bowl with the garlic, mustard powder and salt, and whisk until smooth and combined. Mix together the two oils, then add ½ a teaspoon of the oil mixture to the egg yolk. Mix thoroughly with the whisk, then continue adding a teaspoon at a time until an emulsion forms – this means the egg yolk and oil will combine smoothly, becoming thicker and creamier. After about half the oil is incorporated into the aioli, you can start adding it in larger quantities, a couple of tablespoons at a time. Once all the oil is incorporated, you should have a smooth yellow sauce the texture of mayonnaise. Add the lemon juice and whisk that in, too, then taste and decide if you would like to add more salt, lemon or even crushed blanched garlic.

Salsa Verde

SoF / NF / WF / GF / DF

- a small bunch of flat-leaf parsley leaves
- a small bunch of basil, leaves only
- 4 anchovies
- 1 clove of garlic (blanched in boiling water for 3 minutes if you like a more mellow flavour), crushed to a paste with the flat blade of a knife
- 1 heaped tablespoon capers in brine, drained and finely chopped
- ½ teaspoon Dijon mustard
- 1 small shallot, very finely diced
- 1 teaspoon sherry vinegar or red wine vinegar
- 5 tablespoons extra-virgin olive oil

Making this by hand in a pestle and mortar gives a pleasing chunky texture, but you can, of course, just throw everything in a small food processor – just don't over blitz it. Place the herbs and anchovies into a pestle and mortar, and pummel to a pulp. Add the garlic and pummel a bit more, then stir in the capers, mustard, shallot, vinegar and olive oil. Serve immediately or it will keep in the fridge for a few days, with a thin layer of oil on top.

Labneh

SoF / NF / WF / GF / V

- 200g (7oz) full-fat Greek-style yoghurt
- a pinch of salt

Line a sieve with clean muslin or cheesecloth and set it over a bowl. Mix the salt into the yoghurt, then pour into the lined sieve. Leave to drain in the fridge for 8 hours or overnight. When ready, the labneh cheese will be very thick, having lost lots of liquid. How much labneh you end up with depends on how thick the yoghurt was to begin with – it may lose up to a quarter of its weight in liquid. Labneh will keep in the fridge for 3 or 4 days (or for 1–2 weeks, if rolled in balls and submerged in olive oil).

Pink Pickled Onions

makes 3 × 400g (14oz) jars

SoF / NF / WF / GF / DF / V / Ve

- 3 red onions, very finely sliced

  FOR THE BRINE:
- 200ml (7fl oz) white wine vinegar
- 100ml (3½fl oz) cider vinegar
- 200ml (7fl oz) water
- 2 tablespoons sugar
- 1 tablespoon salt

Wash and dry three tempered (heatproof) glass jam jars with lids, then place in the oven on a low heat for about 15 minutes, to sterilize. Set aside to cool slightly. Pack the onions tightly into the jars. Bring all the brine ingredients to the boil in a non-reactive pan, then remove from the heat and divide the hot brine among the jars. Seal immediately with the lids. Leave the jars to cool, then store somewhere dark. The onions can be used as soon as they're cool, but pickles are best after they've had at least a few days to develop, ideally a week. Once opened, keep in the fridge. Use a clean spoon when taking them from the jar (this will help them keep longer), leaving the brine behind.

Puffed & Popped Seeds

Serves 4 as a topping

SoF / NF / WF / GF / DF / V / Ve

- 40g (1½oz) pumpkin seeds
- 1–2 tablespoons mixture of sesame seeds and flax/linseeds (optional)

Place a frying pan over a medium heat. Tip in the seeds and cook for 2–3 minutes until they begin to pop and puff up in size. Allow the pumpkin seeds to brown just slightly, giving them a nutty flavour, then remove from the heat, making sure they don't burn.

Roasty Toasty Nuts

SoF / WF / GF / DF / V / Ve

- 100g (3½oz) mixed unroasted, unsalted nuts, chopped into pieces if large

If using the oven, heat it to 180°C/400°F/gas mark 6. Spread the nuts over a baking tray and roast for 5–7 minutes, depending on the size of the nuts, until golden. On the hob, set a dry pan over a low heat. When hot, add the nuts and cook, tossing frequently, for 2–4 minutes until brown and toasted. If you want to coat the nuts with spices, you can use either water, water and beaten egg white, or water and melted butter. Just mix a couple of tablespoons of each together with your spices (paprika, sugar, salt, cumin, za'atar, chilli, etc.) and then toss the nuts thoroughly in the mixture before roasting in the oven.

Ciabatta Croutons

SoF / NF / DF / V / Ve

- 300g (10½oz) day-old ciabatta, torn into bite-sized pieces
- 1 tablespoon extra-virgin olive oil

Heat the oven to 200°C fan/425°F/ gas mark 7. Toss the ciabatta pieces in the olive oil and arrange on a baking tray. Bake in the hot oven for 10 minutes, or until the croutons are golden and crisp.

Brioche Croutons

SoF / NF / V

- butter, for spreading
- 200g (7oz) brioche, sliced

Heat the oven to 200°C fan/425°F/ gas mark 7. Butter the brioche, then cut it into 2cm (¾in) cubes. Place the cubes on a baking tray, buttered-side up, and cook for 6 minutes, or until beginning to brown.

Glossary

UK	US
Almonds, flaked	Almonds, slivered
Aubergine	Eggplant
Back bacon	Use Canadian-style bacon or ham
Beetroot	Beets
Broccoli, Tenderstem or sprouting	Broccoli, baby (broccolini)
Butterbeans	Lima beans
Cabbage, Chinese	Cabbage, napa
Cabbage, white	Cabbage, green
Chinese leaf	Chinese greens
Chopping board	Cutting board
Coconut, desiccated	Coconut, dry unsweetened
Coconut cream	Coconut cream, unsweetened (not cream of coconut)
Coriander	If referring to leaves, cilantro
Cornflour	Cornstarch
Courgette	Zucchini
Flour, plain	Flour, all-purpose
Griddle pan, ridged	Grill pan, ridged
Kitchen paper	Paper towels
Knob (of butter)	Pat (of butter)
Lamb's lettuce	Corn salad
Linseeds	Flaxseed
Muslin	Cheesecloth
Pips	Seeds
Prawns	Shrimp
Pulses	Beans and other legumes
Puy lentils	French green lentils
Rapeseed oil	Canola oil
Red mullet	Use red snapper
Rocket	Arugula
Spring onions	Scallions
Steak, rump/sirloin	Steak, sirloin/tenderloin
Stick blender	Immersion blender
Stone	Pit
Sugar, caster	Sugar, superfine
Tea towel	Dish towel
Tomato purée	Tomato paste

Cook's Notes

We have endeavoured to be as accurate as possible in all the prep and cook times listed in this book. However, they are an estimate based on our own timings during recipe testing, and should be taken as a guide only.

Nutrition advice is not absolute. Please consult a qualified nutritionist if you require specialist advice.

Standard level spoon measurements are used in all recipes. 1 tablespoon = one 15ml spoon; 1 teaspoon = one 5ml spoon

All leaves and vegetables should be washed before use.

Eggs should be medium unless otherwise stated and preferably free range and organic. This book contains dishes made with raw or lightly cooked eggs. It is prudent for more vulnerable people to avoid uncooked or lightly cooked dishes made with eggs. Once prepared these dishes should be kept refrigerated and used promptly.

Fresh herbs should be used unless otherwise stated. If using dried herbs, halve the quantity stated.

All oven temperatures are for a fan-assisted oven. For a conventional oven, increase the temperature by 20°C/70°F.

This book includes dishes made with nuts and nut derivatives. It is advisable for readers with known allergic reactions to nuts and nut derivatives and those who may be potentially vulnerable to these allergies, such as pregnant and nursing mothers, invalids, the elderly, babies and children, to avoid dishes made with nuts and nut oils. It is also prudent to check the labels of pre-prepared ingredients for the possible inclusion of nut derivatives.

Vegetarians should look for the 'V' symbol on a cheese to ensure it is made with vegetarian rennet.

Not all soy sauce is gluten-free – we use tamari, which is almost always gluten-free, but do check the label.

If you are cooking for someone with any known allergies, remember to check the labels on ready-made ingredients to ensure they don't contain allergens.

Index

Acknowlegements

LEON

LEON was founded on the twin principles that food can both taste good and do you good. When Henry Dimbleby, John Vincent and Allegra McEvedy opened their first restaurant, on London's Carnaby Street in July 2004, their aim was to change the face of fast food. Six months after opening, LEON was named the Best New Restaurant in Great Britain at the *Observer Food Monthly* Awards (by a judging panel that included Rick Stein, Gordon Ramsay, Nigel Slater, Heston Blumenthal, Ruth Rogers and Jay Rayner). There are now more than 70 LEON restaurants in the UK and the Netherlands. LEON has published more than 20 cookbooks including *LEON Fast Vegan*, *LEON Happy Salads*, *LEON Happy Guts* and *LEON Happy One-pot Vegetarian*.

When we started LEON in 2004, the mission was to make it easier for everybody to eat well, with food that tastes good, and does you good whilst being kind to the planet. Roll forward a few years, we have more restaurants around the UK (and the Netherlands), and we're still dedicated to this same journey.

So we have some thank yous to make to a few people who help make our everyday happen.

Firstly, to our fun-loving managers and their hard-working teams who are the beating heart of LEON, along with the Copperfield Support Team who support them through every step of their days. Without our team's daily efforts, we wouldn't even have a LEON that could publish cookbooks like this one.

Secondly, to you. To every guest who chooses to dine with us in one of our restaurants, who buys a cookbook or a sauce from their local supermarket – thank you.

Finally, thanks to our incredible author Rebecca Seal, and to our wonderful publishers Octopus, who have always been a pleasure to work with. More than twenty cookbooks later, we're proud to be great friends, constantly talking, smiling and planning our future cookbooks together.

So that's that. We're really truly grateful. And we remain servants to the same old LEON question, asking why can't fast food also be good food?

The LEON Family x

Rebecca Seal

Rebecca has written about food and drink for the *Observer*, the *Guardian*, the *Financial Times*, *Evening Standard*, *The Sunday Times*, *National Geographic* and *Sainsbury's Magazine*. Her cookbooks include *Istanbul: Recipes from the heart of Turkey* and *Lisbon: Recipes from the heart of Portugal*, as well as co-authoring *LEON Happy Soups*, *LEON Happy One-pot Cooking*, *LEON Happy Curries*, *LEON Happy Fast Food* and *LEON Happy Guts* with John Vincent, *LEON Fast Vegan* with John Vincent and Chantal Symons, and *LEON Happy One-Pot Vegetarian* with Chantal Symons. Her first non-food book – *SOLO: How To Work Alone (And Not Lose Your Mind)* – was published in 2020. She lives in London with her husband and two small daughters.

It feels like quite a privilege to be able to work with LEON, and to have done so for several years. Very few companies work as hard to do the right things as LEON does, nor are they so well stocked with so many lovely people. Particular thanks to Glenn Edwards for letting me loose on another LEON book, and to Mariam French for all the help and creative input as we put the book together. Erica Molyneux's knowledge of LEON's philosophy, food and past recipes was, as ever, invaluable.

At Octopus, I'd like to thank Alison Starling, Pauline Bache, Matt Grindon and Hazel O'Brien; once again, a dream publishing and publicity team. I am thrilled with Jonathan Christie's fantastic design for this book. Thanks to copy editor Emily Preece-Morrison, and proofreader Emma Bastow, who gently ironed out any wrinkles in the text.

Despite it being a hot one, the shoot was one of the nicest we've done, and the results are just beautiful. Thanks to photographer Steven Joyce and his assistants Tom Groves and Matt Hague, Frankie Unsworth for the deliciously good food styling, Rosie Jenkins for her perfect props, and Rinku Dutt for hand modelling. (Thanks to all of you for letting me appear at lunchtimes, and basically do nothing else of use.)

Perhaps the best bit of writing a recipe book is coming up with the initial ideas, which was all the more fun because we had input from LEON team members across the board. Thanks in particular to Stacey Strachan, Emily-Jane Ruddick, Pinar Seseogullari, Ashley Davis and Jacob Kerr, for their recipes and inspiration. LEON is a team effort, and so was this book.